THE
SNAKE BOOK

Other Books by Roy Pinney

VANISHING WILDLIFE
VANISHING TRIBES
ANIMALS OF THE BIBLE
UNDERWATER ARCHAEOLOGY
CAVE EXPLORATION

THE
SNAKE BOOK

Roy Pinney

Acc · 13334

Zoological Consultant ROBERT PRICE
New York University

Doubleday & Company, Inc.
Garden City, New York   1981

Library of Congress Cataloging in Publication Data

Pinney, Roy.
The snake book.

Includes index.
1. Snakes.   I. Title.
QL666.06P54   597.96
ISBN: 0-385-13547-5
Library of Congress Catalog Card Number 78–68336

9 8 7 6 5 4 3 2

Dedicated to the memory of
Irving Schiffer

Contents

The Herpetologists

Born and brought up on New York's Lower East Side, I knew as a young man one kind of jungle, and dreamed of another. My imagination roamed freely to the tropical jungles and rain forests of W. H. Hudson's *Green Mansions* and the vivid descriptions of Amazonia made by William Beebe. That someday I would walk those jungle trails myself I knew would inevitably happen, when the time came.

My book-nourished "jungle fever" was not restricted to those exotic, mysterious places per se but encompassed the wildlife native to them, with emphasis, of course, on snakes. Snakes in general. The giant anaconda in particular. I think that what probably intrigued me most of all about these reptilian behemoths was the fabric of legend and mystery which had been woven about them over the centuries—and right down to modern times. I read everything I could find in print about anacondas, ranging from unsubstantiated reports to scientifically verified accounts—all relative to length and circumference. I soon found myself distinguishing between tall tales and documented reports. The gap between them was much like that to be discerned between a fisherman's weight estimate of the one that got away and the actual weight of the one sizzling in the frying pan.

And yet—the unverified reports (well, some of them, anyway) made me wonder a bit. Discounting solemnly sworn-to tales of anacondas of 60, 80, 115, and 120 feet still left to be considered reports (some noted in today's *Guinness Book of Records*) of lesser colossi in snakes' clothing. That figure of speech was not as frivolous as it might sound, for further research revealed that many measurements, so called, above the more realistic 27 feet 9 inches probable record length, were taken from the skin. And the skin of an anaconda, or any other snake, is inclined to stretch when re-

The author holding a bushmaster (*Lachesis mutus*), largest of the American pit vipers, found in northern South America and Central America. They reportedly grow to a length of 12 feet, have large venom glands and enormous fangs, making them greatly feared by the natives. This specimen was captured in Panama. (*Photo: Ken Bobrowsky*)

moved from the carcass, perhaps as much as 25 per cent. Add to that some additional stretching intentionally achieved, and you have a snake a half city block long. Well, 45 feet long, at any rate.

One giant, said to be accurately measured at 37½ feet, was shot by a petroleum geologist named Roberto Limón in the Upper Orinoco, near the Colombia-Venezuela boundary. He and members of his party fired .45 slugs at a huge anaconda which soon apparently gave up the ghost. But when they returned later to skin it—no snake. Another one which got away. Others in the 35–45-foot range have been reported in Brazil and Peru but never have any of these "measurements" been substantiated.

Anacondas, I had learned, run to great bulk as well as length and one measuring 20 feet might well weigh 250 pounds, twice that of its nearest rival in length, the reticulated python. Clifford Pope, apparently suggesting that there might be some truth to claims that anacondas reach tremendous lengths, offered the theory that a giant subspecies might exist. This made a certain amount of sense to me at the time, conceding that what amounted to freaks, as of the circus variety, conceivably could exist. I decided that since I was determined to see and get the real feel of the tropical jungle, I might as well (to mix a metaphor) kill two birds with one stone. That is to say, visit the giant anaconda in its own home environment, tape measure in hand. Just in case.

The day finally came. I found myself in Georgetown, British Guiana, as it was called before the country achieved its independence in 1966 and became Guyana. Anthropologist Walter Roth introduced me to Thomas, whom he recommended as the best possible of guides. Thomas and I got acquainted in short order. I hired him, and we began our journey up the Essequibo River aboard a supply-laden launch. He soon dispelled any preconceived notions I had about men of his trade. He was not the Hollywood version of the Great White Hunter, tough, dashing, fearless. Not that he lacked courage. Years of experience had equipped him to handle whatever emergency might arise. He had a large quota of good common sense, and vast experience in the jungle and with its denizens. He was competent, knowledgeable, and unflappable. What more could you ask?

In the decades to follow, I was to chalk up over a hundred expeditions throughout the world, mostly in Central and South America, plus Africa, Afghanistan, Indonesia, the Philippines, and the South Pacific. Yet never was I to experience a more memorable trip than this, my first introduction to the real jungle country of Guyana. The sheer beauty of it all was almost too much to take in. City streets no longer existed. Surely they had been illusory, all that asphalt and concrete. The *castanheiras,* or Brazil-nut trees, towered 150 feet overhead. Birds vied with orchids for unbelievable coloration, and they in turn were challenged by butterflies in that huge green cathedral, its dome studded by tiny patches of cerulean blue sky.

We had stopped at a river trading post; Thomas had directed me to a dry path which led deep into the jungle, sensing, perhaps, that those first steps might best be taken alone. His only word of caution had been to advise that I take note of landmarks so that I would have no trouble finding my way back within an hour, the rendezvous time. Thereafter, following my solitary baptism, we traveled together, and even then, usually in silence, broken only when he would point out something of interest I might otherwise have missed or when I asked a question.

When we resumed our upriver odyssey, I asked what he considered to be the greatest danger in the jungle.

"Falling trees," he replied. I thought he was ribbing me, but he, no doubt noting my expression, continued to say, "I'm quite serious. I have known people to be seriously hurt, even killed, by falling trees, but only rarely by animals. And that includes poisonous snakes. Unless disturbed or provoked, they'd rather go their way while you go yours."

We were in full agreement that the fear of snakes, as opposed to sensible caution, is inculcated rather than innate, and fostered by ignorance concerning their habits. I learned that of the forty-odd species of snakes to be found in Guyana, only seven or eight were poisonous. This discussion, of course, led to anacondas (*Eunectes murinus*), ranging in length, according to Thomas, up to nearly, but not quite, 30 feet. Over the years he had heard any number of claims regarding the sighting and even the killing of super-giants, to 50 feet and longer. When I told him that I had hopes of catching a record-breaking anaconda, his reply was that a full 30 feet would do the trick, but that I'd better not get my hopes too high—or that high.

On subsequent trips to Guyana, I placed advertisements offering $1,000 for a live specimen of that length, and a bonus of $100 per foot above 30 feet. No one took me up on it. Raymond Ditmars, Curator of Reptiles at New York Zoological Park, either more optimistic (or more cautious?) than I, had made a similar offer for a skin which measured over 40 feet. Not even the most skillful of skin-stretchers applied for the bounty.

A record-breaking anaconda there was not, but live anacondas in their natural habitat there were, and that made the trip an unqualified success as far as I was concerned. From our boat we saw sizable specimens on shore—not large enough to swallow the mythical meal of an entire cow, but large enough to enjoy a whole pig as a snack. On one occasion we spotted one slithering into the river, apparently in pursuit of some prey—and quite disdainful of the voracious piranhas in those waters. The anaconda relishes the smaller caimans. One of them might have been the victim of those powerful, constricting coils.

I recall one moment when for a very brief time I entertained hopes of impressing Thomas, and the entire scientific world, for that matter. A report reached me that a 40-foot anaconda had been dynamited out of the depths of the Cuyuni River near the site where William Beebe established his tropical research station. I walked for a full day from Kartabo and purchased the skin—which, when measured, was all of 17 feet 6 inches long. I began to understand how observers on many occasions had seen more snake than was there.

RAYMOND L. DITMARS

To me as a New Yorker, Mecca was the Reptile House of the New York Zoological Society—better known, then as now, as the Bronx Zoo. Its curator, Raymond L. Ditmars, whose renown had been firmly established for many years, was, in my opinion, and that of fellow budding herpetologists, the fount of all knowledge where serpents were concerned. For that matter, his name had become almost a household word to the general public. A prolific and skilled writer, he also was much written about, for he had a way of finding himself in situations which made excellent copy for newspapers and magazines.

One example of this proclivity, an incident which occurred just about the time I had finally worked up my courage to seek out the oracle for information and advice—from the horse's mouth, to mix a metaphor.

The headline in the New York *Times* read roughly as follows:

DITMARS SHARES PULLMAN
BERTH WITH KING COBRA

The text below detailed a dilemma in which Ditmars found himself, how he solved it, and the results. Washington's National Zoo was planning to open a new reptile house but lacked what would be the star of any collection—a king cobra. Ditmars could sympathize. No one knew better than he how hard that spectacular snake was to come by. Then, as though in answer to a prayer which stipulated instant results, he got word that a dealer in New Jersey had just acquired, not one, but two king cobras as part of a shipment from Singapore. Although they were in poor condition—undernourished and bruised—he bought both, one for the Washington zoo and the other for the Bronx collection. By the time the new reptile house in the nation's capital was ready, the intervening weeks of expert care had restored the cobras to their natural splendor.

The next problem on the agenda was how to get Washington's cobra to its destination. It was early winter, and a cold one. Tropical snakes and, for that matter, those indigenous to the so-called temperate zones cannot survive low temperatures. To ship the cobra would entail a freezing journey of many hours, which might prove fatal. Ditmars decided to take it along with him on the sleeper, a feasible plan provided Pullman personnel remained unaware of the contents of their passenger's extra piece of luggage. Yet Ditmars felt it a necessary precaution to label the suitcase: "Caution! Living Cobra En Route Zoo," or words to that effect—just in case the bag was picked up by mistake. Not that he would not take the logical step to prevent such an error by never letting the suitcase out of his sight. The king cobra thus rode first-class, as befitted his nomenclature, even to sharing Ditmars' blanket in the lower berth, and arrived at his new home without incident.

Ditmars was scheduled to give a lecture as well as make the delivery. The Washington zoo director, amused by his guest's initiative, urged that he make mention of it in the course of his talk. This he did. It intrigued not only his audience but the press as well. The story was front-paged, and its readers included executives of the Pullman car company, who in turn wrote a letter of severe castigation to Ditmars, scolding him for allegedly endangering the lives of hundreds of passengers and crewmen from the engineer to the dining-car cook.

Exasperated by what he regarded as uncalled-for hysteria, he fired back with a letter which ripped their arguments to tatters. In some unexplained way this heated exchange became known to one of the major airlines of that era, the head of which saw excellent public relations value in urging Ditmars, whose colorful activities always drew a good press, to make use of their facilities at any time—man, snake, or both. Needless to say, delighted reporters pounced on this one, too.

Thus it was, with this story in the back of my mind, that I had a preconceived image of Ditmars when I first called upon him at his office. But instead of the fun-loving prankster I had visualized, I found myself confronted by a man of serious, even brusque mien which bordered on the outright formal. However, the lack of that quality known as cordiality or an easygoing manner soon became of no consequence whatever. Ditmars' door was always open to his often awestruck young disciples. He had ready and ungrudging answers to our questions and gave encouragement when it seemed merited. I realize now that he was always more than generous with his time and great knowledge, especially in view of his time-consuming duties, both *in situ* at the reptile house and with his heavy schedule of lectures, collection trips, and film making.

Raymond Ditmars' boyhood passions, aside from snakes, ever his number-one obsession, included meteorology, fire engines, and collecting butterflies. It was his expertise in the latter which, incongruously enough, was a prime factor in opening the door to what was to become a lifelong career as a herpetologist. His parents were adamant in their initial refusal to tolerate the presence of live snakes in their home. Mounted butterflies had their sanction, however, and also sparked the interest of Dr. William Beutenmüller in young Ditmars when he showed a framed example of mounted moths to the American Museum of Natural History scientist. Ray was hired to work on the museum's collection. But his overwhelming interest in snakes soon made itself felt. Though but seventeen, he wrote a paper on snakes in Central Park which he delivered as a lecture before a museum association audience. He was encouraged by such eminent museum staff heads as Professor Henry Osborn, zoologist Dr. William Hornaday, and William Beebe. Dr. Beutenmüller suggested that he enlarge the report to cover snakes of the entire state. Ditmars did so and it was published. This was his first great step ahead in his chosen field. Even his proud parents lifted their ban on snakes about the house, never dreaming, it may be presumed, that an entire floor of their home would be infiltrated by reptiles, including poisonous ones.

Another great experience for young Ditmars was receipt at the museum of a request from a Port-of-Spain, Trinidad, herpetologist, one R. R. Mole. Mole offered a collection of snakes from his area in exchange for an equal selection of North American specimens. Ray was more than delighted to swap a shipment of rattlers, copperheads, various adders, black racers, and indigo snakes for pairs of emerald and coral snakes, a bushmaster, fer-de-lances, boa constrictors, and other tropical prizes. He housed the lot in glassed-in cages on the top floor. When he became interested in antivenins, it became a laboratory as well, where he "milked," or extracted, venom by pressing the snake's fangs against a chamois-covered glass, into which the poison, hypodermic fashion, was injected.

Little by little, the name of young Ditmars and word of his activities were spreading. A newspaper article on his study of snake venom resulted in a visit from the distinguished Dr. Weir Mitchell, who was a pioneer in the search for effective antivenins. His interest gave great impetus to Ditmars' investigations in an area which at that time was very little advanced. He could not, however, afford his collecting and research on his salary from the Museum of Natural History. His next move proved, paradoxically, to be a step higher toward, rather than away from, his elected career. He left the museum to become a reporter on the New York *Times*. After a period of routine assignments he was asked to interview his old acquaintance Dr. Hornaday, of the New York Zoological Society and the new Bronx Zoo-in-the-making.

Ditmars found Hornaday's enthusiasm for the project contagious, and his resultant story in the *Times* inspired an offer from Hornaday to be Keeper of the Reptiles, as assistant curator of the zoological gardens in the Bronx. Ditmars' personal reptile collection numbered 45. It became the nucleus of what was to be a total of 400 by year's end. He further rounded out his capabilities by sewing back together a disemboweled alligator, which lived for another thirty years. His skill as a doctor was further demonstrated when he healed the mouth of a reticulated python, then cured the snake of a stubborn refusal to keep down food by turning a hose on it. He also patched up the loser in a cobra vs. cobra battle, removing a section of diseased jawbone.

Meanwhile Ditmars was working on his book, based on notes he had taken for several years. *The Reptile Book,* dealing with North American species, was scientifically accurate, yet comprehensible to laymen. If there remained an achievement to establish his permanent niche in the scientific world, this was it. The year was 1907. The zoo was drawing immense crowds. Teachers brought their classes to view and learn. The reptile collection by now numbered nearly 900 specimens. Two years later Ditmars made a European tour and returned with four dozen cases of reptiles, birds, and mammals; the range of his expertise extended well beyond the confines of snakes.

Collaboration with Brazilian scientists and the exchange of North American snake venom for antivenin (their serums could not be sold in the United States but could be "given") led in time to antivenin manufacture in the Mulford Laboratories in Pennsylvania. Widespread dissemination of instructions for treating snakebite slowly but surely cut down the mortality rate.

Ditmars had been augmenting his lectures with a "vaudeville" display of small creatures, but only species which were easily portable yet large enough to be seen by the audience. Thus many creatures as large as polar bears and elephants and those too tiny to be readily visible (such as tadpoles, and their life cycle) had to be omitted. Ditmars solved the problem with a comparatively new invention— the motion-picture camera. So successful were his films that commercial motion-picture companies bought and showed them—many decades before Marlin Perkins' TV films were regarded as an innovation. Ditmars, by now married and a family man, achieved another dream—the construction of a large home in Scarsdale, New York, which included a fine movie studio. Andrew Carnegie was so impressed by a private showing of Ditmars' films that he contributed $100,000 to the Zoological Society's pension fund.

Although most of Ditmars' collection trips extended over an area within two hundred miles of New York City, he did on occasion extend his scientific travels as far afield as California, Panama, Honduras, Brazil, and the Mediterranean, plus Trinidad. There he was given the unique honor of having a calypso song extolling his activities composed and performed. He continued to give lectures, and never relaxed in his efforts not only to spread knowledge and understanding but to advance the work of the Antivenin Society. How many lives he was directly or indirectly involved in saving, and how many lives he enriched through sharing his findings, will remain incalculable.

ROSS ALLEN

Like many another herpetologist, Ross Allen became fascinated with snakes when he was still a small boy. In fact, by the time he was twelve, he had established his own "museum" of reptiles at home. If his parents found this a discomfort, they nevertheless refrained from discouraging his avid interest. His father, a newspaperman and advertising specialist, entertained hopes that the boy might be inclined to seek a career in the Fourth Estate. However, even though young Allen himself may not have realized it at the time, the die had already been cast.

True, he devoted much of his time and energy to activities such as swimming—he won many trophies and became a high school coach, and a lifeguard in Winter Haven, Florida—and even studied engineering for a while, which was a complete departure. Yet he had continued with hikes and camping trips, had captured his first diamondback rattler and alligator at age sixteen, and earned his college tuition as a part-time taxidermist, which was at least peripheral to what was to become his life's work.

In 1928 Allen enrolled in the Red Cross aquatic school at Brevard, North Carolina, and mastered the art of canoeing, a skill which was to stand him in good stead on future reptile-collecting trips. The following year, with the cooperation of W. C. Ray and W. M. Davidson, he founded the Ross Allen Reptile Institute at Silver Springs, near Ocala, Florida. Initially, it was a tourist attraction, featuring exhibits of snakes of the area, such as diamondbacks, water moccasins, copperheads, and coral snakes, plus other reptiles—principally alligators, crocodiles, caimans, and turtles ranging in size up to the giant alligator snapping turtle. In time, mammals were added and a Seminole Indian Village shared billing with the many other attractions.

Allen found that he had an innate talent for showmanship. He excelled at handling and displaying his "stars," but his forte proved to be an exhibition of feinting for position with, seizing, and milking the venom from giant diamondback rattlers. Many imitated but none equaled his showmanship in this department. The extraction of venom had a more basic value than just entertaining the visitors. Allen became an expert on snakebite and its treatment, and pro-

Ross Allen with an eastern diamondback rattlesnake (*Crotalus adamanteus*), demonstrating its large fangs. (*Photo: Ross Allen Associates*)

duced venom for antitoxin conversion by commercial laboratories. The venom was processed and dried in the reptile center's laboratory and shipped to hospitals, doctors, and pharmaceutical houses.

Allen also has written extensively for scientific journals, fishing and sporting magazines, and conservation journals, and in these areas probably surpassed his father's fondest hopes that he would make a reputation for himself in print. As a talented performer, he caught the attention of motion-picture producers, and starred in approximately forty film feature shorts. The size of the live audience he entertained and educated over the decades at Silver Springs can hardly be estimated. By the time he shifted operations to a location near St. Augustine, Florida (The Alligator Farm), Allen had already succeeded in a lifetime career as a widely recognized naturalist and herpetologist, and might have retired with his laurels. But the only change is that in his surroundings, and he is an institution as much as the one he founded forty-odd years ago.

BILL HAAST

"What! wouldst thou have a serpent sting thee twice?"

That line, lifted completely out of context from *The Merchant of Venice,* poses a question which might well have been put to Bill Haast of the Miami Serpentarium some three decades ago. Just about that time he sustained his first bite from one of the horde of venomous snakes which he harbored and exhibited for the delectation of gaping and gasping tourists.

His answer, immediately after being detoxified, was to go right back to work, risking (and receiving, in due time) not only the second bite, but the tenth, the fiftieth, the one hundredth, and, according to the latest report at hand, number 138. A confirmed masochist? Myopic? Just plain clumsy or careless? No indeed. Haast is none of these. His being bitten so many times over a period of thirty years is in fact testimony to his courageous dedication to as dangerous and selfless a career as any man might choose—that of supplying medical science with snake venom for research purposes.

When Haast opened the Serpentarium back in 1948, it was primarily a roadside attraction, but not for long. By 1950, modern science was conducting experiments which promised to confirm the conviction of the ancient Greeks and Romans that snake venom has curative properties. This intrigued Haast, and he volunteered to supply venom for research into polio, journeying to Southeast Asia and Africa in quest of Malayan pit vipers and cobras. Two hundred of the former died in an epidemic, but the cobras survived and became the star attraction at the Serpentarium.

The polio research was making headway, but the vaccine discovered by Dr. Jonas Salk swept away all competition. Haast, not to be

At his Miami Serpentarium in Florida, Bill Haast daily demonstrates to crowds of open-mouthed spectators how venom is obtained from cobras and kraits. (*Photo: Charlotte Bourdier/Haast*)

deterred in what had become his near-obsession to contribute to medical science (it was already obvious that he would be risking death on a daily basis), went to work himself—and on himself. He began injecting himself with neurotoxic cobra venom, diluted one to ten thousand, and gradually increasing the proportion of venom until after one year his system was absorbing the equivalent of one drop—sufficient to kill any other man. In this way he built up his own immunity, not only against the cobra but against many other lethal snakes as well. His collection, now numbering 1,200, became a principal source of venom for the laboratories (he produced half the world's supply). He continued to take the venom by hand, grasping the snake directly behind the head and forcing it to bite through a porous membrane stretched over a glass receptacle. This was dangerous as well as slow and tedious work, with little profit apart from the satisfaction of knowing that his venom factory's product, which he converted into a stable powdered form at a low cost, was making a vital contribution to the treatment of many human ills, as well as snakebite.

His self-immunization program provided him with a high level of resistance, although at times, and especially during the early years, somewhat less than 100 per cent. Hospitalization was required from time to time, although no extreme measures were ever necessary. On the other hand, Haast has been flown to the bedsides of snakebite victims again and again, to give of his blood, which has become more effective, because of its antibodies, than other serums. The Serpentarium became more laboratory than showplace, but in order to keep the project going, Haast has continued with his "duels" with cobras, climaxed by milking them. Admission fees helped subsidize the serum production.

Meanwhile researchers were finding new uses for the venom, as an analgesic for pain and as both a coagulant and an anticoagulant. Such dramatic findings were a source of great satisfaction to Haast, making threats to his own health seem secondary in importance. There remained one episode, however, which probably would have been chilling enough to make anyone else have second thoughts.

Haast had received bites from the Mexican moccasin, the diamondback rattlesnake, and both Indian and Egyptian cobras. He made an expedition to India and returned with live specimens of the blue krait, fifteen times as venomous as the dreaded cobra and responsible for a terrible toll of life. In fact, there had been but one instance of a survivor from its bite on record. Shortly after an injection of combined Indian cobra, African Cape cobra, and king cobra venom, Haast attempted to draw the venom from the krait. He was bitten on the back of the hand. Panic would have been pardonable, especially in view of the frightful box score of the krait. But Bill Haast, after returning the snake to its cage, merely applied disinfectant, told his wife what had happened, and managed to calm her by example. He scorned the traditional procedures such as slashing the wound and using a tourniquet. After all, the antivenin in his blood had pulled him through many a crisis before. He simply sat back to wait, well aware that physical movement and excitement only serves to increase the spread of the venom throughout the veins.

Two hours passed and he still felt perfectly well. He got busy with some paper work, and then began to experience mild euphoria. He had been bitten by the krait at four that afternoon. By seven-thirty he was feeling high as a kite and insisted on keeping an appointment to immunize some hunting dogs. His wife, by now quite aware that he was by no means himself, was distinctly worried and tried in vain to dissuade him. (He admitted later that by the time he was ready to leave the house his arm had become sore, as had his throat, and he felt much less like making the trip.)

He reached his destination, saw to the dogs, but noted that locomotion had become difficult; he was quite unsteady on his feet. As he drove back home his vision became blurred and mild hallucination set in. He had to prop one eyelid open in order to see. Mrs. Haast wanted him to call a doctor, but he refused, stating that a doctor could not help him. His body ached all over. Vomiting and chills came as no surprise to him, but other symptoms indeed did. His hearing became tremendously amplified, he was unable to swallow, and could breathe only through his mouth. Colors seemed intensely brilliant. He asked for pencil and paper, to note down his symptoms for possible research use. Even in his most extreme moments, his mind remained clear and he felt keenly that this experience was as valuable as it was rare from a scientific standpoint.

Despite previous orders to the contrary, his wife called the hospital and spoke to a research technician. He came to the house, recognized the symptoms of shock, and made several emergency calls. Haast was taken to the hospital, where he was examined by several doctors, including Dr. Murray Sanders, an expert in venom research. However, like all others available, he had no specific knowledge of what course to follow in a case of krait poisoning. While hurried calls were placed to Bombay, Haast received conventional treatment, including a tracheotomy to alleviate his breathing difficulty, and intravenous feeding.

The doctor in Bombay was incredulous on receiving the news that a man bitten by a krait eighteen hours previously was still alive—and without injections of krait antivenin. He could offer no professional advice as to specific treatment at this stage, but did volunteer to rush antivenin by air.

Aside from neurological symptoms—and new and most unusual ones kept appearing—Haast's life signs and blood count, as well as urinalysis, were pronounced to be normal. But as he lay motionless, his muscles hard and rigid, he experienced all the hallucinations that today are referred to, in connection with LSD, as "a trip." Vivid colors, time and space warps, and, in general, mind-expanding "experiences" kept invading his being, ever-changing and beyond rational description. These aberrations were of a highly pleasant nature and Haast enjoyed them to the fullest.

The krait antivenin arrived, but it was in such a moldy condition that it had to be discarded. However, the neurological aberrations and other symptoms began to wane after thirty-six hours. Against the wishes of his physicians, Haast insisted on being discharged and on the third day he was taken home.

The following day he was back at work, convinced that if he could survive the bite of a blue krait (*Bungarus caeruleus*) he could survive anything. Furthermore, it seemed evident that this strange venom, once made available to the research laboratories, might yield valuable secrets to science. In his correspondence with Stanford University and Walter Reed Hospital he urged that the *Bungarus* toxin be broken down. He went to Taiwan and wound up with nearly 400 kraits and ever since has been supplying the venom, which may yield a remedy for lateral sclerosis and other human ills. Haast still thrills the crowds, but his real career is the pursuit of knowledge to the benefit of mankind.

L. G. PILLSTROM

L. G. Pillstrom, as a graduate student at the University of Arkansas, enrolled in a herpetology class in 1953. At that time the conventional method of catching reptiles was to use a forked stick, a pole with a right-angle iron, or leather straps in the form of a loop at the end of a stick. None of these was very acceptable to the future doctor who sought a safer way to catch snakes for study.

This started Pillstrom thinking about an easier and safer method. He got a mop handle and a piece of wire and began to experiment. Since he didn't have tools to heat and bend metal, part of a refrigerator shelf was used to fashion a crude affair that had jaws. It was made of strips of angle iron at one end and a sort of trigger at the other. By using a spring, the jaws could be opened at will. But the first rig was too weak.

Next he obtained some aluminum tubing to use for the barrel and an L-shaped piece for the handle. The rig still used the jaws which closed with the use of a spring. He experimented further, and found that thirty-six-inch tongs proved best. The final version of his present streamlined catcher.

With about seventy of these packed in the car, Pillstrom and a fellow med student set out for Okeene, Oklahoma, to attend the annual rattlesnake roundup. All were sold before the pair left the roundup. With a patent pending, Pillstrom made an agreement with a firm to manufacture the tongs out of heavy-duty aircraft aluminum. The tongs are suitable for catching snakes, lizards, small alligators, turtles, and frogs.

CARL KAUFFELD

What do you suppose a zoo employee does on his vacation? You might expect that after eleven months of constant daily contact with animals he would want to get as far away as possible from the sight, smell, and sound of these creatures. But this is seldom the case. Like the proverbial busman on holiday, curators hew to their occupational interests while on vacation. Carl Kauffeld, formerly the Curator of Reptiles and later the Director of the Staten Island Zoo in New York City, would drive a thousand miles or more to collect snakes and I would often accompany him.

I first came to know Kauffeld in the early 1930's. Still in our teens, we were assistants to G. Kingsley Noble, of the Department of Herpetology, American Museum of Natural History. Dr. Noble held that the proper approach to the study of snakes was to examine preserved specimens, so we spent many rigorous hours transferring them from one jar of alcohol or formaldehyde to another, very nearly pickling our hands in the process. But we did learn how to identify and classify many species by counting scales and making other anatomical comparisons.

Carl Kauffeld capturing a Gila monster (*Heloderma suspectum*). (*Photo: Roy Pinney*)

At the age of nine, when most boys dream of becoming a fireman or a major-league baseball star, Philadelphia-born Kauffeld came across a copy of *The Reptile Book* in the family library and his goal in life was set. A scant six years following his apprenticeship at the Museum of Natural History he was named the Staten Island Zoo's first Curator of Reptiles.

Under his direction that zoo became the first to display rattlers indigenous to Aruba, Netherlands West Indies, a new species of Mexican rattlesnake, the first Malayan cave snakes ever to be viewed in an American zoo, as well as Willard's, Twin-spotted, and Rock rattlesnakes.

Rattlers were Carl's prime passion. However, he captured, over the years, a variety of other snakes, never finding it necessary to look beyond the limits of the continental United States. He found domestic hunting grounds every bit as productive as any so-called exotic tropical country. One of his favorite hunting spots was the coastal forest tract in South Carolina maintained by the Okeetee Club as a game preserve. It was my privilege to accompany him there several times.

It may seem an anomaly that an immense area of flatlands, prepared and kept up at great expense for over a half century for the purpose of supporting quail and other game fowl, should prove a paradise for "snakenappers." But natural conditions altered to favor one form of wildlife often can prove an equal boon to others. In this case, a great scattering of small areas was planted with corn, following partial burning and clearing of underbrush and tree stumps— remnants of the original timber, long since felled. The corn not only provided forage for quail but attracted rats, rabbits, and other small mammals and continues to do so. In turn, rodents serve or, one might say, are served up as welcome meals for snakes, who, somewhat like "the man who came to dinner," feast and stay on, ensconced in the labyrinth of tunnels previously inhabited by their hosts. Stumps, hollowed out like volcano craters, still retain their elaborate root systems and, in many cases enlarged by their original tenants, provide both homes and escape routes. Spring and the first rays of sunlight sufficient to create any perceptible warmth will be the signal for snakes to end their hibernation period and emerge from their dens. And, accordingly, we snake hunters from ours.

I remember my first South Carolina junkets with Kauffeld and,

from time to time, in the excellent company of Carl Herrmann and
Bill Summerfield as well. As was customary, we launched the season
by making a call on the Okeetee clubhouse, where the superin-
tendents, N. Burton Bass and his son Robert, and the warden, Harry
Bennett, always gave us a warm welcome—and useful information.
It was Mr. Bennett who, two years previously, had shown Carl what
he considered a likely spot for diamondback rattlers. Carl, in turn,
wanted to show it to me, and as he described his adventures there,
with the enthusiasm of a fisherman sharing his knowledge of a secret
place where trout "that long" jostled for the honor of striking his
lure, I was only too happy to accept the invitation. As we drove
along a narrow dirt road, past stands of pine, white oaks draped
with Spanish moss, and occasional patches of swamp, he made clear
his gratitude to Warden Bennett.

On that memorable April morning, two years before, the wind,
anathema to snakes wherever they may be, was a mere gentle
breeze. The sun's rays were pale, but yielded enough warmth to per-
suade snakes to leave their subterranean lurking places. And any
one of the numerous stumps might well prove to be just that. However, a giant windfall, or tree felled by a windstorm, somehow
demanded attention first. Carl approached quietly, for a heavy foot-
fall can cause earth vibrations which would frighten any potential
quarry right back into his hole. The fallen tree proved to be a windfall in more ways than one. Stretched out on the trunk, near the
bramble-covered roots, lay a large and resplendent diamondback,
rendered almost invisible by the crosshatch pattern of interlacing
shadows which blended with his markings.

Carl reached out with his long-handled snake hook and flipped
the surprised creature, staccato rattle sounding, onto the ground. Immediately he adopted the classic diamondback defense, coiled, lung-
ing again and again, but all the while retreating—a motion which
makes it possible to back a diamondback into a waiting collecting
bag.

One year later, give or take a few days, Carl returned to the same
windfall, if only to recall exciting memories. But on that trunk there
lay, as though time had not passed at all, a very large diamondback
rattler. Slightly dazed with surprise, he bagged it—and on his way
back to the car, found a fine corn snake half hidden by dry leaves at
the base of a stump.

As we neared this remarkable site, I could not help but suggest that he was stretching his luck a bit by hoping to find another diamondback, making it three in a row. He agreed. But you've guessed it. Three in a row it was. Another big one—and another even taller tale, which happens to be the truth. And it was my great pleasure to be in on the finale, for such it was. Three times and out, but Carl never complained.

Another productive place, where there were three mounds of sand (known in Okeetee country as "hurricanes" since they had been tossed up by roots of trees felled by winds of hurricane force), produced, on one fine hunting day, a pair of mating hognose snakes. Well known for their fake attacks, followed by "playing possum" if threatened or touched, this pair had more difficulty than normal in rolling over on their backs, since first, of course, they had to separate.

Our hunting was not restricted entirely to stumps, logs, and fallen trees, hollow or otherwise. One day Carl spotted part of the coiled body of a rat snake on a tree branch some twenty feet from the ground. We found a long, sturdy pole. Carl Herrmann, normally a loner who preferred to hunt by himself but was still with us that morning, positioned himself under the branch. Carl gave the snake a calculated shove, and even before it had time to uncoil it landed in Carl Herrmann's firm grasp—as neat a piece of fielding as I have ever seen.

Then, not far from the state road, situated between two cornfields, we came across bits and pieces of what once had been a cabin. Corrugated metal, evidently from what had been the roof, afforded not only protection from the wind but warmth, à la hot tin roof—ideal for basking snakes. There Carl found a five-foot corn snake and a black racer, just for openers. That metal refuge yielded, over a period of three seasons, three more corn snakes, two black racers, one coachwhip, one small diamondback, and two garter snakes.

Another site where man had lent an unwitting assist to nature was a forest edge where traces only, in the form of railroad ties (the rails had long since vanished), remained of what once had been a railroad spur which hauled timber to mills in Savannah, thirty-five miles to the south. Pine planks had been placed to make it possible for trucks to cross the old road bed. Beneath slabs were found copperheads, kingsnakes, ringneck snakes, marbled salamanders, and skinks—all told, a dazzling and variegated display of reptilian life.

But diamondback rattlers remained at the top of Carl Kauffeld's list, something I readily could understand. They are, indeed, the big game of our snake population.

C. J. P. IONIDES

My visit to Nairobi in the summer of 1968 was made memorable by a highly enjoyable meeting with C. J. P. Ionides, the legendary Snake Man of East Africa. A fifth-generation Englishman of Greek descent, he abandoned a brief military career in favor of becoming, by turn, a professional big-game hunter, a game ranger, and a dedicated herpetologist. He had only recently returned from a snake-catching expedition in Indonesia. I purchased several superb specimens from him for my personal collection, including king cobras and mambas. Then, business out of the way, we settled down to snake talk. I had read his memoirs, *Mambas and Man Eaters: A Hunter's Story,* with keen interest, and as a consequence was all the more eager to become acquainted with this remarkable man.

A quarter century before, L. S. B. Leakey, the famous anthropologist and curator of the Coryndon Museum in Nairobi, had expressed a need for additions to his snake park there. Young Ionides had always been interested in snakes ("on their side," as he put it), but never had had the time to give them much attention. His decision to take the assignment proved to be a major turning point in his life.

His first catches, he recalls, were a garter snake and a night adder, which he shipped by parcel post to Leakey. He used a forked stick, the most primitive of tools, and still wondered how he got along with nothing safer and more efficient, for quite some long time. His next prize was what was to be the first of some thousands of mambas, in this instance a black mamba—a snake which attains a length of nearly 11 feet in the area where Ionides was hunting, and is as powerful as it is venomous. He pounced with the stick, pinning what could be seen of his quarry at a point which proved to be the exact middle of its back. Thus he found himself confronted with two four-foot lengths, anterior and posterior, which flailed wildly about, the business end striking repeatedly in the direction of Ionides' hand. Happily, the stick was long enough, though just barely, to prevent his being bitten. He finally pinned the head of his adversary to the ground with a section of rotted log, then grabbed head and neck with his weather-beaten hat giving him purchase. There ensued a battle royal, with the neophyte snake catcher the ultimate victor as he manhandled the mamba into a wire-fronted box.

The forked stick, which had served well enough with small, less poisonous or nonpoisonous snakes, was, quite obviously, less than reliable for pinioning more lethal and muscular catches. Ionides devised an adaptation embodying a noose—an improvement which later on was further improved upon by a grab stick constructed along the lines of the device once employed by grocers to retrieve wares from out-of-reach shelves. Considerable skill and strength were nevertheless still necessary.

It seems unlikely to me that any other snake catcher in Africa, or elsewhere, for that matter, could have acquired as profound a knowledge of such a variety of snakes as Ionides. As for mambas, on one safari alone he accounted for 123 of the black variety, whose venom is so deadly that two drops will kill. Over a period of a few years he captured more than 3,000 green mambas and large numbers of Jameson's mambas. In relating his experiences with these and many other species, he carefully differentiated among them as to haunts, habits, degrees of aggressiveness, and even personality traits. Ionides was also an expert on snakebite.

Among the victims he quite candidly included himself. In his early days he was bitten on two occasions by burrowing adders, vipers that jab with extremely long fangs which project below the lower jaw. He blamed both misadventures on lack of experience. In relation to its body the burrowing adder's head is very small and can swivel or gyrate very rapidly. The manner in which he seized it might have served with other snakes, but the adder nailed him, and for eight days he suffered from severe swelling and discoloration. He reasoned that this bite may have served him well some years later, in providing immunization from a second bite. In any event (he had mistaken a burrowing adder for a small snake which it resembles), his discomfort the second time was minimal.

The puff adder, another viper even more versatile in striking from unexpected directions, is blamed for more deaths in Africa than any other snake. Nevertheless, Ionides once captured a female who raised no objections at being handled, and he kept her in a box with the idea of taming her. At first, they got along quite well, but then her good nature deteriorated. When he fetched her along to a dinner party to demonstrate to visitors from England how to handle a poisonous snake, she promptly sank a fang into his forefinger. End of lesson, and end of the adder as a pet. His arm swelled to the elbow, and so it remained for more than a week. His by then ex-pet was "decanted," as he put it, into the bush.

Among the serpents which Ionides encountered, studied, and had unpleasant confrontations with was the spitting cobra. The largest captured by him measured 7 feet 5 inches, perhaps not in the same league with the king cobra of the Far East, but most certainly to be reckoned with because of the talent hinted at by its name. This snake can face prey or attacker and eject two fine sprays of venom for distances up to ten feet and more. The poisonous mist can cause temporary blindness and, in any event, excruciating pain. On one occasion while in Somaliland, Ionides, observing a spitting cobra in action, from what was considered a safe distance, caught some of the spray in one eye. He adopted the obvious countermeasure, washing out the eye, which furnished some but rather little relief. Fortunately a doctor was available; he used a medicinal eyewash and administered a sedative, which proved effective, though leaving Ionides with a sore eye for many days.

Another time, failing to get his protective goggles in place before a spitting cobra raised its hood and let loose, he reduced the pain considerably with a solution of potassium permanganate. Presumably, the four molecules of oxygen contained in the salt formed a compound with the venom and neutralized its effect. In both cases Ionides was lucky in that only a small quantity of the mist reached his eyes. It might be added at this juncture that if Ionides appears to have been careless in the course of the aforementioned mishaps, it is well to bear in mind that he learned his lessons in the surest way there is—the hard way—and that throughout the years which ensued he caught and handled several thousand dangerous snakes without injury.

When he was forced by ill health to retire from his post as game ranger and give up his hobby of hunting for rare animals, he turned to snake collecting as a full-time activity. Among his remarkable finds were four hitherto unknown species and several subspecies, including a very rare small two-headed snake. Constantine Ionides became a name known to herpetologists the world over, and orders for snakes and venom poured in. Employing a Land-Rover, and a single-wheeled rickshaw when forest paths were impassable with a motor vehicle, Ionides pursued his vocation all over East Africa. He found this new life exciting and extremely rewarding in all respects. Added to his long list were Egyptian cobras, black forest cobras, water cobras, and Gaboon vipers, rhinoceros vipers, and saw-scaled vipers, all in quantities ranging into the hundreds.

Ionides was primarily interested in poisonous snakes, though he did go after pythons. These, however, often were so huge that they posed problems in handling and packing which he found not quite worth the struggle.

Until the end, which came a few months after my meeting with him in Nairobi, Constantine John Philip Ionides used his home in Newals, Tanzania, near the Mozambique border as a base from which he could operate daily, with all the zeal and enthusiasm which characterized him. He had achieved his great goal, the capture of king cobras, during that final summer in 1968. He had often been quoted as saying that if he caught a king cobra, he could then die happy. And so it was.

CLIFFORD POPE

The hills of home, and the fields and swamps where small boys explore, often serve as training grounds for tomorrow's career naturalist. Certainly thus it was with Clifford H. Pope, born in the small town of Washington, Georgia. All the varied forms of wildlife he encountered and came to know sparked an interest which was to shape a long and distinguished career as a herpetologist and writer on the subject.

Shortly after receiving his Bachelor of Science degree from the University of Virginia in 1921, young Pope learned that Roy Chapman Andrews, under whose aegis the American Museum of Natural History was organizing an expedition to Asia, was looking for an assistant. He applied for the position, was hired, and soon thereafter found himself in the eastern half of China, much of which had never been herpetologically explored. The objective was to secure and preserve a representative collection of mammals, fish, and reptiles. By this time, Pope's main interest was in snakes, and so highly was his knowledge and experience regarded that he was put in charge of independent investigations and relieved of the duties of general assistant.

During the years 1921–26, Pope and his Chinese helpers combed seven provinces, including Fukien and Kuatun, concentrating on his chief interest, reptiles and amphibians. Since few of his assistants knew English, he applied himself to learning Chinese, which proved invaluable not only in communicating with them but in questioning the natives. Pope and his team worked in a wide variety of surroundings and situations, aboard houseboats, in temples and ancestral halls, mission compounds, Chinese homes, and, routinely, in American tents. He became accustomed to the native diet, and when in the remote mountains where local food supplies were nonexistent, relied on canned goods and wild meat. The latter included the flesh of cobras and pythons, which, especially in the course of snake-hunting activities, were plentiful.

The terrain was rampant with vegetation. A semitropical to tropical climate provided ideal conditions for snakes and, accordingly, fine hunting for the herpetologist. The commonest method of capturing snakes was the simplest one: the quarry was picked up with a long stick and popped into a canvas bag. Specimens most frequently taken included pit vipers, cobras, coral snakes, kraits, and pythons.

The Chinese locals preferred their own unique procedure for collecting snakes, which they sold to the expedition. Rather than employ bags of cloth, they improvised containers on the spot which usually consisted of bamboo poles or makeshift bags made from large leaves. The pole method was ingenious in concept at least, although at times it lacked in efficiency and posed certain problems. The wriggling captive had to be tied to a length of bamboo with cord made from a strand of rope or grass. After a few contortions it would become difficult to tell where the string ended and the snake began, or ended, as the case might be. Such contests caused more than a small amount of excitement, to say nothing of amusement.

Pope reported an ingenious device that Chinese natives used for capturing and pinioning snakes. A bamboo rod, its tip partly split down the middle, amounting to the traditional forked stick, was employed after the manner of spring-powered, long-handled tongs. Once the victim was pinned, the tips, thus far held open by a small block, were allowed to close and the snake was powerless to wriggle free.

The activities of the expedition spelled bonanza to the locals wherever Pope and his assistants went. Everyone, children included, had word via the grapevine that these strange men were in the market for snakes, and they acted accordingly, offering specimens at a wide range of prices. Pope would pay an initial top price for the first "round" of any particular species, and then pay a bit less for each successive one. This served to stimulate competition, in that the hunters had to speed up their work before the market price dropped on the day, or days, following. Needless to say, this system worked and captured snakes turned up in satisfactory abundance.

Quite naturally, in country where snakes were so numerous, snakebite was common and treatment by various methods, all of them traditional, was a widespread and active business. Village shops, the equivalents of apothecaries, were in fierce competition with their arrays of bottles of colored solutions. Medicine men set up stalls in the cities and displayed large charts purporting to demonstrate how various parts of the body reacted to the venom of various serpents. At times a bottle would contain the repelling, partially decomposed remnants of the snake itself. While all of this obviously reeked of quackery, it is interesting to note, as did Pope, that the use of snake gall was highly recommended. While such a primitive belief was scorned by civilized Western medicine, it was later discovered that snake gall does indeed contain an ingredient which is effective against snakebite.

At one time during Pope's long stay in China, he had a base of operation aboard a rented houseboat on the Yangtze River in the vicinity of Ningkwo. It was here that a most interesting discovery emerged—a new snake, *Elaphe bimaculata* (nomenclature by Dr. Karl Schmidt). This species had been collected previously, but never before recognized as distinct from *Elaphe dione,* one of the commonest snakes of northern China.

From the standpoint of behavior, perhaps the most fascinating species to turn up in the Ningkwo region was the so-called two-headed snake (*Calimaria septentrionalis*). The head and tail of this species are nearly identical in shape and color. Pope recalled that a captive specimen, when held by the tail, continued to try to escape, but when pinned down by the head, the entire body was hurled forward, wrapping itself around the restraining fingers, the tip of the tail repeatedly pressed against them. The tail apparently was taking the offensive, thus not only mimicking the head in form and color pattern but in behavior as well.

By the time Pope left China, thirty-five forms of snakes had been collected, six of them proving to be new to science.

On his return to the United States, Pope was signed on by the American Museum of Natural History as an assistant in the Department of Herpetology, advancing to the post of Curator in 1928. Aside from scientific papers, he wrote the occasional article for popular magazines, developing a literary technique that was to serve him well later on. By 1934 he completed assembling the text and illustrations for his definitive work, *The Reptiles of China,* which was published the following year. In 1935 he left the museum to devote himself to magazine articles and a book called *Snakes Alive and How They Live,* still in print three decades later. He had mastered a style which, while embodying all his encyclopedic knowledge, including that of his years in the field in China, avoided technical jargon and was highly readable to the student and layman.

In 1941 Pope joined the staff of Chicago's Field Museum as Curator of Amphibians and Reptiles, a post which had been vacated by Dr. Karl Schmidt, who had long been an enthusiastic supporter of Pope. There he served for twelve years until his death, a period during which he wrote prolifically, both for periodicals and as author of numerous successful books, including his *Reptiles Round the World* and *The Giant Snakes,* both of which were reprinted in Great Britain. He wrote less of his own discoveries in field and laboratory than he did of the work of others, and with a scientific exactitude and clarity which greatly enlarged the scope and dissemination of herpetological literature.

A Vocational and Occupational Hazard

When snakebite puts an end to a human life, who is the victim likely to be? The barefoot native in India, the careless camper, the amateur collector not quite on the qui vive? The answer is any and all of them, and more. But, you may ask, what about the professionals, the skilled herpetologists who handle venomous snakes with their bare hands, time and time again, over the years? Does not their expertise safeguard them against "the wily serpent"?

Usually, yes. Always, no.

KARL P. SCHMIDT

It was the afternoon of September 25, 1957. A thirty-inch snake had been brought from the Lincoln Park Zoo to the Chicago Museum of Natural History for identification, and Karl P. Schmidt, Curator Emeritus of the museum, was being consulted. Robert Inger was holding the reptile with a firm grip directly behind the head, in the prescribed manner. The head shape, coloration, and formation of the scales all were characteristic of the African boomslang, or tree snake (*Dispholidus typus*), but the anal plate was undivided. The latter contradicted the established morphology of the boomslang, and the scientists were puzzled. Dr. Schmidt took the snake from Dr. Inger for a closer look, grasping it by the neck, just behind the other scientist's fingers. Freed of the pressure behind the head which had immobilized it, the snake twisted and bit Schmidt's thumb. One of the rear fangs made a small mark; the other penetrated its full length of about three millimeters. A few drops of blood surfaced, but there were no more immediate symptoms.

Dr. Schmidt sucked at the wounds; he and his colleagues were not unduly alarmed, for the boomslang (which now it obviously was, though an aberrant type) was young, presumably was able to inject only a small amount of venom, and that with but one fang. Also, although Dr. Schmidt was sixty-seven, he was in good health. But a short time later the thumb began to swell, and it was evident that it might have been advisable to inject antivenin immediately after the bite occurred. Ever the true scientist, he decided to keep notes on changes in his condition, and began this aboard a surburban train on his way home.

During that hour of travel he was afflicted with nausea, and upon arrival home experienced chills and a fever. He was bundled in blankets, with a heating pad, and bleeding from the gums commenced at about five-thirty that afternoon. He managed to sleep from nine until a little after midnight, when his urine was mostly blood. Bleeding from the mouth had continued at a low but steady rate, and there was severe abdominal pain. During the rest of the night there was continued nausea and vomiting.

At seven the following morning, Dr. Schmidt reported additional bleeding, this time from the bowels. By ten o'clock, however, he felt well enough to telephone the museum and advise he would report for work the following morning. But by noon he experienced great difficulty in breathing. The family physician and an inhalator squad were summoned. First attempts to resuscitate him appeared successful, but it soon became apparent that his condition was worsening. He was taken to the hospital and died there shortly before three o'clock that afternoon, approximately twenty-four hours after the boomslang bite. An autopsy revealed massive internal bleeding and multiple brain hemorrhages.

It was painfully evident that Dr. Schmidt not only had invited the fatal strike by absentmindedly grasping the snake in a careless manner, but had also seriously underrated the potential of its venom, which is even more toxic than that of the dreaded krait, mamba, and cobra. Here was an eminent zoologist and herpetologist, upon whom many signal honors had been conferred over a period of some forty years, who met an agonizing end because of a momentary lapse of caution, compounded, perhaps, with overoptimism.

GRACE WILEY

Grace Wiley, who lived with her eighty-four-year-old mother in the little town of Cypress, California, overcame her fear of snakes as a schoolgirl in Kansas and came to love them. Her attempts to enter the field of herpetology as a professional failed on two occasions, and for the same reason. When she was Curator of the Museum of Natural History at the Minneapolis Public Library, her way of handling venomous snakes was considered reckless, a danger to others as well as herself. She then was hired by Chicago's Brookfield Zoo, again to be criticized on the same grounds.

In time, she moved on to her own roadside home-cum-serpentarium in Cypress, where she maintained and at times exhibited a fine collection, including diamondbacks, fer-de-lances, Egyptian and king cobras, the deadly kraits, and vipers from Italy. She had gained a wide reputation for having a way with snakes bordering on the magical. Her starring role was with a large king cobra, and it was truly a hair-raising performance, even to "snake people" long accustomed to handling the most dangerous of reptiles:

As the cobra watched, she would move her hand in its direction, the head swaying and following as though preparing to strike—as indeed it was—this puzzling target, which, after a few lazy-looking but carefully calculated passes, moved directly above its head as the hand lowered itself. By this time the cobra's hood was fully extended and the serpent was hissing. Onlookers were covered with gooseflesh as Grace Wiley tried to touch the hood and the snake struck—but missed. Barely.

That would seem like sheer bravado, if not suicidal. Yet every move she made was with complete assurance. She knew, of course, that she had the advantage of position. A cobra cannot strike vertically, directly above its head, as a rattlesnake and other venomous snakes can. Yet she went a step further, extending her open palm at an angle from which the cobra could, and did, strike, but with its mouth shut, not once but several times and making repeated contact, more rapidly than you can drum on a tabletop with your forefinger.

Why was her hand untouched by bared fangs? Because, as she well knew, the cobra could not gain a prize on the flat surface of her hand. It needed a target, such as a finger, upon which it could close its jaws and bite as venom flowed into the open wound. A king cobra is not equipped with hollow fangs, as, for instance, a rattlesnake is, and cannot pierce, then inject poison, on the principle of a hypodermic needle. Nevertheless—allow a cobra to strike, perhaps gambling on the off chance that it might seize the edge of the palm? Russian roulette it was, to the observer certainly, but not to Grace

Wiley, at least as far as she was concerned. And there was yet more to come:

With perfect calm and sureness she would then slide her open hand over the king cobra's head and stroke it. At first the snake would hiss and struggle violently in protest, but then slowly submit, until the hood closed. Then she would gently lift the snake and cradle it in her arms, unperturbed as its tongue darted in and out, directly in front of her face. In some strange way she imparted her own calm to the cobra, which she then would lower gently into its glass-fronted cage.

One day she received a shipment of cobras from Siam, as it was then called. One of the snakes had a mark on its hood which closely resembled the letter G. Since this was her initial, she decided that it had been marked for her. And thus it proved to be, bearing out in a tragic equivalent the old saying of soldiers—that the bullet which gets you has your name or your initials on it.

A photographer who was doing an article on Grace Wiley came to the house to take shots of her posing with her new "monogrammed" acquisition. She decided that she would photograph better without her glasses, and removed them. Then she extended her palm toward the cobra, and, as anticipated, it struck. But this time, it was not according to the many-times-played script. The cobra found her middle finger and seized it. She disengaged the fangs quite calmly, returned the snake to its cage, and only then did she indicate where she kept her snakebite kit. A crude tourniquet was applied to her wrist, though much too late, and an injection of strychnine was administered as she lay on the floor. A herpetologist friend was called. He arrived, along with a hastily summoned ambulance. Blood transfusions and an iron lung were made ready, but a half hour later she died—some ninety minutes after the cobra had bitten her.

Were the movements of this cobra different, in millimeters and split seconds, from those to which she had been accustomed, and had always adjusted her timing so perfectly? Might she have avoided the fatal strike if she had kept on her glasses? It could have been one of those factors, or the other, or a combination of both. No one can say, no one can ever know.

Thus far we have explored in some detail the cases of an eminent professional herpetologist and a semiprofessional and gifted snake lover; now to that of a physician so knowledgeable that he was considered a leading, though but part-time herpetologist.

FREDERICK A. SHANNON

Frederick A. Shannon of Wickenburg, Arizona, some fifty miles northwest of Phoenix, was inspecting some property outside the village of Klondyke when he encountered two miners, who told him they had seen nearby what they were certain was a Mohave rattlesnake. He decided to attempt to capture it, and walked to the spot indicated, together with two young relatives, who later related to Shannon's colleague, another herpetologist, what happened.

Dr. Shannon had first told his companions that the Mojave rattlesnake (*Crotalus scutulatus*) was perhaps the most deadly of all U.S. venomous reptiles, and gave them instructions as to what measures to take in the event he was bitten. He then poked about in the area with the stick, finally overturning the stone under which the snake had taken refuge. Immediately upon being exposed, it lunged and struck Dr. Shannon on a finger of his left hand. He turned and staggered toward his car, collapsing as he neared it. The nearest hospital was an hour away, in Stafford, where he was driven. Antivenin and a blood transfusion were administered. The physician attending him knew of Dr. Findlay Russell, associate professor of neurosurgery at Loma Linda University, a friend of Dr. Shannon and a fellow herpetologist. He also was a recognized authority on snakebite. An open-line telephonic conference was begun at once and maintained over the next fourteen hours. Dr. Russell gave professional advice, but the patient's condition deteriorated to the point where it was arranged to fly him to Los Angeles General Hospital by ambulance plane.

Although the case seemed hopeless, a team of ten surgeons began open-heart massage and monitored his condition via electrocardiography for three quarters of an hour, but in vain.

Dr. Shannon had written many papers on snakebite and was a member of a National Academy of Sciences committee on snakebite; their report (Dr. Russell was chairman of the committee) was later incorporated into the Desert Survival Manual of the Armed Forces. Knowledgeable? Obviously. Careless? On the contrary. He had sought out the snake with commendable caution. The answer, if any, is that it is impossible to be *too* cautious when dealing with venomous snakes, which, in the aggregate, are assailants of infinite patience, ever looking, like a prizefighter, for the one opening of a millisecond.

Physiology

WHAT IS A SNAKE?

A snake is a lizard modified for eating large prey. It is essentially a long flexible tube which expends little energy on anything other than procuring and digesting food and reproduction. As such, snakes exhibit less intelligence than many lizards and, usually, limited complicated instinctive behaviors, such as territoriality or socialization.

A snake seldom has to eat more often than every few weeks, and can elude predators quite efficiently even though it lacks legs and arms. The girdles which support these appendages in other animals would block the passage of large food objects.

The snakes are the newest of all reptile groups, having evolved near the end of the Cretaceous period some 100 million years ago. It is doubtful that the first snakes were able to eat whole objects as large as those modern snakes consume. To consume and digest large prey, snakes had to develop such things as constriction, venom, and a body habitus that allows them to hide efficiently while digesting.

It is thought that the first snakes evolved either in grasslands or underground. In such environments, legs obviously would have been an impediment, so they were gradually lost. The loss of legs allowed for large food objects to pass down the gastrointestinal tract. However, dramatic modifications of the lizard skull and jaw articulation also were necessary. Whether underground or in grasslands, snakes lost the external ear, which also would have been an impediment, and developed the spectacle to protect the eye from injury.

Boid-type snakes (pythons and boas) apparently emerged at the end of the Cretaceous or during the early Tertiary period, some 65 million years ago. They had the power of constriction. Venom, which did not develop until much later, is largely a device to subdue

The garter snake (*Thamnophis sirtalis sirtalis*) and its related forms, probably one of the most familiar groups of reptiles of North America, range from southern Canada to Florida and west to Minnesota.

They are particularly fond of frogs but will also eat toads, salamanders, earthworms, fish, etc. Young are born alive and may number as many as one hundred, the average litter being about half that number.

It is a well-adapted "long flexible tube" which expends little energy on anything other than procuring and digesting food and reproduction. (*Photo: Pinney/Chase*)

and digest large prey. Venom glands developed from salivary glands. The defensive properties of snake venom are a secondary development. Among the components of venom are several potent digestive enzymes, including proteinases and amino acid oxidase.

In short then, a snake is a modified lizard which has sacrificed many skeletal structures, including legs, and has modified many others, including the articulation of the jaw, to become a specialized eating machine for engulfing large objects.

SKIN

The skin of snakes is specialized for two basic purposes: water conservation and protection. During the course of evolution, as reptiles evolved from amphibians, the obvious differences in the skin were primarily concerned with water conservation, allowing reptiles virtually complete freedom from aquatic environments. The snake's skin protects it from attack, disease, and many toxic substances; it may afford a degree of structural support as well.

The skin of snakes consists of raised scales which are composed of thin dead cells filled with keratin. These usually overlap to some extent, and may be smooth or keeled. The scales of the belly are very often modified into large rectangular segments called ventral scutes. In the vast majority of snakes there are nine special scales on the head, called the crown scutes, which are often used to typify many species and higher classifications. They are larger than the other dorsal scales. Between the scales there is some flexible, soft skin which may be seen in a snake that has stretched itself temporarily by swallowing a very large food object.

It has recently been learned that the scales of different snakes show a myriad of strange patterns under the electron microscope. These are consistent for each species, and are of some value in determining relationships between species and higher taxa.

Beneath the aforementioned layers of skin lies the dermis, which is well developed in snakes. It is made up largely of fibrous connective tissue and contains most of the pigment cells responsible for a snake's color, as well as most of the skin circulation. Among the cells of the dermis are melanophores, cells which can lighten or darken the skin by concentrating or dispersing their dark pigment. Closer to the surface are the guanophores, which account for blue color, then still closer and almost at the epidermal border are the lipophores, which produce yellow. Allophores are uncommon pigment cells which are not found in many species. They produce red, violet, and orange hues.

The skin of a snake does not contain many glands, but there are a few that should be mentioned. The cloacal glands of garter snakes are probably the most notorious; these produce the offensive odor which is used as a defense mechanism. Some species of snakes have glands on the skin of the neck which may function in sex recognition.

SKIN PATTERNS

The geometric elegance of a snake's scales catch the eye, but what of the evolutionary significance of reptile skin? Desiccation on the land was a major obstacle to be overcome by the first reptiles. Just as the shelled, amniotic egg prevented drying out of the embryo, so the scaly nonporous skin served to protect the animal later in development. The basic structure of scales would in the course of evolution become modified into the feathers of birds.

The color patterns of many reptiles change through the life of the individual. Most frequently, juveniles have brighter, clearer patterns than the adults.

The colorful and intricate patterns seen on the Gaboon viper (*Bitis gabonica gabonica*) of Africa combine blacks, browns, yellows, purples, and buffs. The potpourri of geometrical designs blends in so well on the forest floor that it may be difficult to clearly discern the snake's body outline from a distance of but a few feet. (*Photo: Roy Pinney*)

SCALELESS SNAKES

The surface scales of snakes are one of their characteristic means of identification. Each scale projects backward to overlap the one behind. The scales are formed from thickened areas of the keratinized integument (covering of the body or skin) which grow up and backward and become hardened. Periodically a new set of scales forms beneath the old and when this happens the outer, older covering is shed. Snakes turn the skin inside out as they shed it, whereas lizards simply creep out of the old skin, leaving it right side out, or shed it in flakes.

A unique specimen of gopher snake (*Pituophis melanoleucus catenifer*), lacking dorsal and lateral body scales, was used to evaluate the physiological importance of reptilian scales—specifically, their role in reptilian water loss and heat transfer. The conclusion of the experiments by Paul Licht and Albert Bennett at the University of California, Berkeley, seems to cast doubts upon the assertions that scales are an adaptation to retard water loss or that their presence is significant in convective heat transfer.

The scaleless specimen was collected near Oakland, California.

ALBINISM

A white blacksnake? Not unusual, according to Kenneth Bobrowsky. Several such snakes have been recorded in scientific literature. Cases of albinism in the black rat snake, corn snake, and other species are also on record.

An albino is an organism (plant or animal) that lacks all body color pigment and, in the case of animals, has pink or red eye color. Varying from complete albinism there may be found degrees of light-colored pigment and body color patterns. The definition describing the degree of albinism is largely open to individual interpretation. Body patterns in most albino specimens are usually evident, and apparently are caused by lighter-colored pigments such as red or yellows being present. Underlying blood vessels may be seen through the almost transparent skin, and may be a factor in apparent color-pattern formation.

Many so-called albinos are not true albinos, says Bobrowsky,

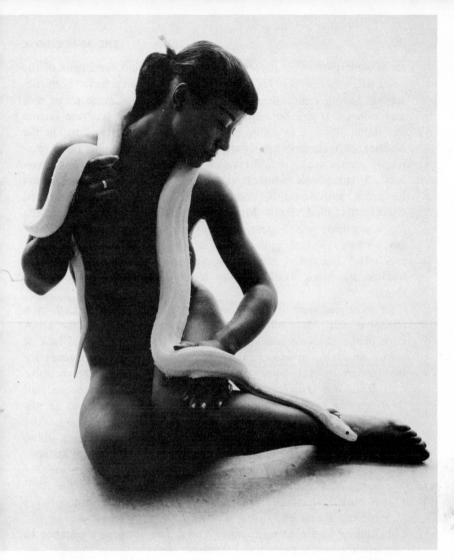

Serata, an 8-foot white rock python from India, became world-famous when she was brought to the United States by Peter Ryhiner, a well-known animal dealer.

Serata was not an albino. She was a color freak in which the guanophores (white pigment cells) exist to the exclusion of all other pigment cells. This condition is known as "leucistic." Serata was aboslutely pure white and no markings of any kind were discernible. With an albino the markings can still be seen as a faint pattern. (*Photo: Roy Pinney*) since some pigment is present in the body. Albino specimens of the northern water snake (*Nerodia sipedon sipedon*) have been described having a reddish eye and a banded pattern made up of reds and yellows. It can be assumed that at least three separate factors determine albinism in water snakes—black, red, and yellow. In the absence of melanophores (parts of the cell containing black pigment) such a snake would take on a colorless or albinistic appearance. A true albino (which is very rare) would lack all three factors for color, and would be completely colorless, except for the red color in the blood vessels. Many snakes classified as albinos lack the black pigments and appear as "colorless" albinos. However, there are probably just as many cases in which such specimens would lack either the red or the yellow pigment color, and go unnoticed because the black would tend to mask the absence of the lighter shade.

In most instances it is believed that albinism is inherited as a recessive trait. Many separate factors or genes (part of the DNA code of the chromosomes) may be responsible for the total lack of color. An albino specimen, then, is one that carries two genes for the absence of each color. Genetically, albinism is a pure recessive trait. Thus if two albino snakes of the same species were bred, all their progeny would be albinos. Other factors in addition to hereditary ones are thought to cause some cases of albinism.

One may ask, even though infrequently, why are there no albino populations? The scientist has formulated the following assumptions:

(1) A pure white reptile would lack protective coloration to protect it from predators.
(2) Linked to albinism, in many cases, is a lowered resistance to environmental factors and diseases.
(3) The chances of one albino reaching maturity and mating with another albino of the same species are exceedingly small.

The genetic explanation for albinism or for color production is complex and varies with different types of animals. Colors of animals (black, brown, red, yellow, and their various shades) are known to be formed by the oxidation of colorless chromogens. The reaction requires one or more enzymes to bring it about. As an example, we may add the enzyme tyrosinase to the colorless amino acid tyrosine and produce a dark melanin pigment. Other amino acids may also act as chromogens and be converted to colored substances in the presence of an appropriate enzyme bringing about oxidation.

Serata, the 8-foot white rock python, shared her cage with a normally colored specimen at the Staten Island Zoo in New York City. (*Photo: Staten Island Zoo*)

According to H. Bernard Bechtel's summation in the *Journal of Herpetology* (1978, pp. 521–32), albinism can be produced by:

(1) Defective cell differentiation in embryonic neural crest
(2) Defective migration of chromatophores from neural crest
(3) Defective synthesis of protein in the melanophores
(4) Abnormal phenylalanine metabolism
(5) Lack of tyrosine
(6) Lack of tyrosinase
(7) Presence of tyrosine to melanin inhibited
(8) Copper deficiency in diet
(9) Absence of tyrosinase inhibitors

The following is a partial listing of North American species of snakes in which albinos have been recorded:

Nonpoisonous Snakes

Lichanura trivirgata roseofusca—coastal rosy boa
Cemophora coccinea—scarlet snake
Coluber constrictor—black racer
Diadophis punctatus—ringneck snake
Elaphe guttata—corn snake
Elaphe obsoleta—rat snake
Elaphe vulpina—fox snake
Farancia abacura—mud snake
Heterodon platyrhinos—eastern hognose snake
Heterodon simus—southern hognose snake
Lampropeltis getulus—common kingsnake
Nerodia sipedon—northern water snake
Phyllorhynchus decurtatus—spotted leafnose snake
Pituophis melanoleucus—pine snake
Storeria dekayi—brown snake
Storeria occipitomaculata—redbelly snake
Thamnophis radix—plains garter snake
Tropidoclonion lineatum—lined snake

Venomous Snakes

Crotalus adamanteus—eastern diamondback rattlesnake
Crotalus atrox—western diamondback rattlesnake

Crotalus horridus—timber rattlesnake
Crotalus viridis—western rattlesnake
Micrurus fulvius—coral snake

The incidence of albinistic specimens is related to the prevalence of albino genes in a population. It would be expected therefore that the incidence of albinos would be more frequent where inbreeding

An albino corn snake (*Elaphe guttata*). This beautiful red or orange snake, subject to considerable individual variation in color, ranges from southern New Jersey to southern Florida and southern Louisiana. (*Photo: Ray Faass/Baltimore Zoo*)

The California kingsnake (*Lampropeltis getulus californiae*) comes in two patterns, a striped and a ringed version, with a variety of intermediates. The same brood may have several of each, but in the albino pictured the ringed variant is discernible. (*Photo: San Diego Zoo*)

takes place in isolated populations. Some authorities claim that albinism is not as rare as most of us believe. In San Diego, C. B. Perkins has managed to back-breed a pure albino strain from a single albino female, stating that albinism occurs in from 1/10 to 1/100 of 1 per cent of the offspring in a given population.

Since man first interested himself in wild animals, the individuals exhibiting color abnormalities have possessed a peculiar fascination. Primitive peoples often attributed supernatural power or import to such individuals. The "moon children" of the San Blas Indians in Panama vary in pigmentation but in general the skin lacks all pigment and is horribly blistered by short exposures to sunshine. Those I have seen seldom smiled, avoided bright sunlight, are said to be slow in gait and lack endurance in physical contests. They are retarded in developing sexually and evidence other physiological and psychosomatic behaviors that deviate from the norm. True albinism has been reported for many animals, including the woodchuck, prairie marmot, pocket gopher, muskrat, beaver, porcupine, rabbit, squirrel, bat, deer, sambar, shrew, mole, and sea lion. Among the birds affected are loons, gulls, sora rail, snipe, woodcock, quail, turkey, various owls, crow, raven, robin, bluebird, and several of the finches. Fishes such as brook trout, flounder, eels; also salamanders, frogs, and toads are known to have albino individuals.

Over 100 albino corn snakes have been hatched at the Baltimore, Maryland, Zoo according to Frank Groves, Curator of Reptiles. The albinos are identical in pattern. All have pink eyes, a pinkish white ground color, and very light red body blotches. None shows any trace of black pigmentation. The natal skins were cast about a week after being hatched and the albinos begin feeding on newborn mice, most doubling their original weight in four months.

A wild-caught female albino black rat snake was mated with a normal male, four years later, to produce six heterozygous offspring. By interbreeding the offspring and mating one of them back to the albino female, seven more albinos were produced at the Baltimore Zoo.

MELANISM

Melanism is usually a matter of the degree to which the dark pigment appears much blacker than the normal coloration. L. M. Klauber recognizes two kinds, the first involving the continued presence of many black, or almost black, individuals in a population otherwise not distinguished by being conspicuously darker than neighboring populations that do not produce melanos. This type of melanism is usually ontogenetic, or developmental, for the individuals destined to be black as adults are normally colored at birth. The second type involves only a very few species and may, like albinism, be the result of some chance genetic disturbance that may appear in one or several individuals and then be eliminated from a population.

Among the rattlesnakes, the first kind of melanism occurs among the eastern massasaugas (*Sistrurus catenatus catenatus*). These rattlesnakes ordinarily are quite dark-colored, but with a conspicuous pattern of squarish brown or black blotches on a gray-brown ground color. In some areas, however, many individuals are uniformly black, although the pattern is sometimes faintly evident in different densities of black. The young, including those born to melanistic mothers, are normally colored.

SHEDDING

The scales and the outermost layer of tissue connecting them are called the horny layer, or stratum corneum, of the skin. It is this part which is shed, usually in a single piece. The epithelial tissue of which the stratum corneum is composed is constantly being formed in the next layer down, the stratum germinativum. When a snake is approaching shedding time, the outer layer begins to loosen from the inner, newly formed layer. This results in a clouding of the eyes and a general lessening of color contrast in the skin. The cells which have divided off from the stratum germinativum lose their neural and circulatory connections with the old outer layer, and lymph fluid intervenes between the old and newly forming skin. The actual shedding begins when the jugularis muscle contracts, causing a rise in blood pressure which affects the veins of the head. This swelling in the head region causes skin breakage, usually in the lip area. The snake then rubs against some rough object to remove the old stratum corneum. This period of actual shedding, called ecdysis, may last a few hours. The new skin which has formed under the shed layer is in every way virtually identical to its predecessor. The frequency of shedding in snakes varies greatly depending on rate of growth and age. Young snakes may shed more than once in the course of a month, older adults perhaps only once or twice a year.

TENTACLES

A single species of the tentacled snake (*Erpeton tentaculatum*) possesses a pair of short erectile tentacles on its head, the function of which has long been debated. The two scaly appendages on either side of the tip of its snout were once thought to act as lures for attracting fish, but it is now believed that the highly innervated tentacles function to detect vibrations in the waters of Southeast Asia, where this snake lives.

A curious pair of organs known as the organs of Cuvier, which dissection of the tentacles and the surrounding region disclosed, were found to contain many small processes known as Deneuve bodies, which produce a unique chemical substance that has been identified as triethylphenacotryptamine-hycannabinol, or TEPH.

TEPH serves as an ionic chemoreceptor, and may be used by *Erpeton* to first detect, and then reject as food, fish infected with metal boximia, which usually proves fatal to snakes.

STRUCTURE OF THE RATTLE

The substance which makes up the sections of a rattle is a protein called keratin, the same protein which makes up human hair and fingernails. External structures made of keratin are very common in the animal kingdom, but the evolution of the snake rattle remains a

A novel exhibit for visitors to the Staten Island Zoo, who can hear the rattle by pressing a button that activates an electrical vibrator. (*Photo: Jack Muntzner/Staten Island Zoo*)

mystery. Some herpetologists believe that a mutation occurred in snakes which vibrate their tails (as kingsnakes do) when annoyed, and that this mutation led to the evolution of rattle segments which can make more noise. Some biologists believe the danger of being stepped on by animals with hooves made the evolution of the rattle a mutation that was selected for, and developed ultimately into the complex rattle of modern snakes.

The first-known picture of a rattlesnake was in a book (Rerum Mediarum Novae Hispaniae Thesainus seu Plantarum Animalium Mineralium Mexicanorum Historia) by the explorer Francisco Hernández published in 1628. It depicted the rattle carried with the wide side parallel to the ground. The rattlesnake actually carries its rattle with the wide side perpendicular to the ground. It can bend up, but not down, from its resting position.

The rattle is attached to fused vertebrae in the tip of the tail, and there are muscles present at the site of attachment which allow the snake to vibrate its rattle. The rattle produces sound because each segment grips the one ahead of it firmly enough to stay attached, but the attachment is loose enough to allow vibration against adjacent segments. A young rattlesnake which has not yet shed has only a single rattle button, and therefore cannot produce a sound. Very often in older snakes, parts of the rattle become loose and break off. A rattlesnake adds a segment to its rattle after each shed. As a result of differential growth (resulting in more or less frequent shedding) and rattle breakage, rattlesnakes of the same age often have different numbers of segments in their rattles. In the case of the Santa Catalina rattlesnake (*Crotalus catalinensis*), the genes which code for the rattle are defective, and as new segments are grown, they are promptly lost with the shed.

EARS

As it does in most higher vertebrates, the ear serves major roles in the hearing and equilibrium of snakes. The tympanic membrane (eardrum), middle ear, and eustachian tube are not present in snakes, however. The inner ear consists of three semicircular canals, a utricle, a saccule, a lagena, and a cochlea.

The ability of snakes to perceive sound waves had been questioned until quite recently, as they possess no tympanic membrane, and the columella (sound-carrying bone) instead articulates with the quadrate bone of the jaw. It was long thought that snakes could only perceive vibrations which travel from the ground to the jaws to the columella to the fluid-filled inner ear, where cochlear sensory cells are stimulated. It is now known that colubrid snakes can hear aerial sounds and are moderately sensitive to frequencies of 100 to 700 cycles per second.

The semicircular canals, the saccule, and the utricle function in the maintenance of equilibrium. Movement of endolymph fluid in the inner ear stimulates hair cells in the sensory patches which cause transmission of nerve impulses along the vestibular branch of the auditory nerve to the brain. The semicircular canals, utricle, and saccule are arranged so that different sorts of movement affect different patches of sensory cells, the resulting stimuli making the animal aware of its position and movement.

EYES

Although chemical perception is a most important sense in snakes, most species have fairly good vision, and the sense of sight is quite important even in many nocturnal snakes.

The eyes of snakes apparently evolved from a lizardlike ancestor which became specialized for either burrowing or living in grassland habitat during the end of the Mesozoic Era. As a consequence, the eye of the snake is quite unlike that of any other reptile, and indeed is unique in the animal kingdom. As in most vertebrates, there is an iris which controls the size of the pupil, a cornea and a lens which focus images on a retina, and an optic nerve which carries impulses to the brain. The eyes of snakes differ with respect to the mechanism of near-vision focusing. In all mammals and other reptiles, the shape of the lens changes for visual accommodation. In snakes, the lens is actually pushed forward for visual accommodation; this is accomplished by contraction of the iris which puts pressure on the vitreous body of the eyeball, displacing the gelatinous substance of the vitreous body so that the lens is moved.

Most snakes have only rod cells in their retinas, and therefore see only black and white. Diurnal species usually have round pupils, nocturnal species vertically or horizontally elliptical pupils. A fovea (area of color-sensitive cone cells) is known to occur only in two

The green tree viper (*Trimeresurus gramineus*) is reportedly the leading cause of snakebite accidents in Taiwan, Java, and Thailand. Persons picking tea, cutting bamboo, or clearing undergrowth are most often injured. Fatalities are unknown among adults, but have been reported in children. (*Photo: M. V. Rubio*)

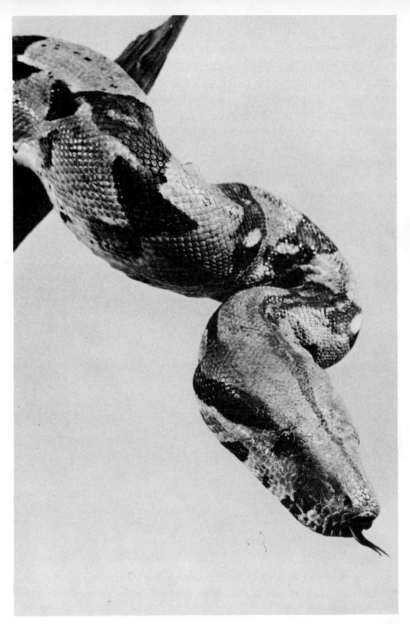

The vertical pupil of the *Boa constrictor* shows that the eye maintains a perpendicular when the head is tilted up or down. The two-toned iris shows the condition seen in many snakes where the colors of the iris conform to the surrounding portion of the head, permitting the patterns to continue uninterruptedly throughout the eye. (*Photo: Roy Pinney*)

species of snakes, the long-nosed tree snake (*Dryophis mycterizans*) and the rear-fanged bird snake (*Thelotornis kirtlandii*). These two snakes have elliptical pupils and grooves along their snouts which work like rifle sights. The groove, pupil, and fovea are lined up, giving these snakes the best vision and depth perception of all serpents. Diurnal snakes have yellow filters in their lens to keep out shorter wavelengths of light.

A retina which contains many rods is more sensitive to light than is a pure-cone retina. If the pupil of a pure-rod or rod-and-cone eye were not capable of closure, dazzle would result in moderate illumination. The animal would be handicapped—at the very time when

The long-nose tree snake (*Dryophis mycterizans*), with its elongate head and body and slender tail, is admirably adapted for its arboreal habitat. It can move with incredible speed both on the ground and through the foliage of trees and shrubs. When at rest, it is able to remain rigidly motionless for long periods of time. Like the boomslang, this mildly venomous snake bites and holds on to its prey until the victim is subdued. Its diet consists of birds, lizards, and frogs. It is found in Ceylon, India, Malaya, and Indonesia. (*Photo: Roy Pinney*)

all its faculties are needed—if routed out of a dim retreat by a diurnal enemy. Basking and sleeping in bright light would be impossible.

Snakes have no nictitating membrane, a thin membrane capable of being drawn across the eyeball, nor do they have eyelids. Instead, they possess a smooth, clear, curved scale called a spectacle, which covers the eye and is shed with the rest of the skin. The spectacle is formed during the development of the snake embryo when the embryonic eyelids fuse. The spectacle protects the eye from protruding objects and during burrowing keeps dirt out.

Since the spectacle keeps the snake's eye from being able to move very much, the field of vision is largely dependent on the position of the eyes on the head. Arboreal snakes which actively hunt in trees need a wide field of vision, as in the vine snake (*Oxybelis aeneus*). This snake can see up, down, forward, and behind, and has binocular vision where the individual fields of each eye overlap in the front. The large protruding eyes of the Trans-Pecos rat snake (*Elaphe subocularis*) provide a wide field of vision and are associated with nocturnal feeding.

Many of the blind snakes (superfamily Typhlopoidae) have much-reduced eyes which can only perceive shadows or barely tell light from dark. These snakes have no distinct spectacle, and only a single kind of visual cell in the retina.

TEETH AND FANGS

There are three types of fang arrangements in venomous snakes. In rear-fanged snakes (opisthoglyphs), there are one to three enlarged teeth on each side of the back of the upper jaw which are grooved and specialized for injecting venom. In most cases, this method of envenomation is not very efficient, and the snake must chew its victim to embed the rear fangs. The opisthoglyphous condition is considered primitive in the evolution of venom apparatus. Many of our common snakes which are harmless to man are, in fact, rear-fanged. Among them are all the black-headed snakes, the vine snake, the lyre snake, the night snake, and the hognose snake. The venom of these snakes is weak. However, the venom of the African boomslang, another rear-fanged snake, can be fatal to man. Most of the rear-fanged snakes are colubrids.

The venomous elapids (proteroglyphs) have a pair of fangs on

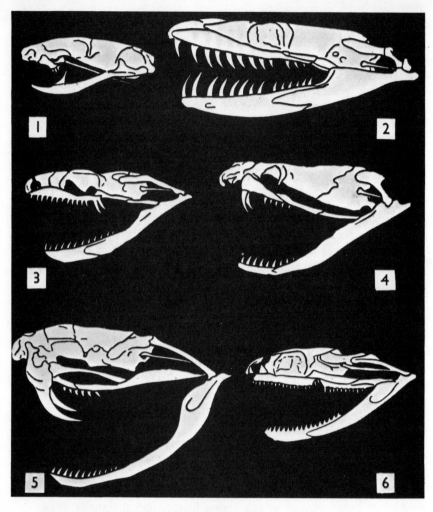

Skulls of snakes showing types of dentition:
(1) Blind snakes: only microscopic teeth
(2) Pythons: long, recurved, solid teeth, no fangs
(3) Brown tree snake: fangs at rear of maxillary bone
(4) Death adder: fangs at front of maxillary bone and followed by several other small teeth on the same bone
(5) Vipers (rattlesnakes, etc.): one large fang only on each maxillary bone
(6) Green tree snake: solid teeth, no fangs
(*Illustration: J. R. Kinghorn*)

the front of each side of the upper jaw (maxillary bone), but usually only one is functional on each side at any given time. These teeth are usually grooved, but may have calcium covering the groove to form a tube. The fangs of proteroglyphs are in a rigidly erect position and fit into depressions in the outer gum of the lower jaw. The fangs are surrounded by a sheath of mucous membrane which is connected to the venom gland by the venom duct. When the snake strikes, a muscle surrounding the venom gland contracts and forces venom through the fang. Proteroglyphs have a few regular teeth on the back of the maxillary bone. Among the better-known proteroglyphs are the coral snakes, cobras, mambas, kraits, and sea snakes.

Solenoglyphs, the vipers and pit vipers, have the most advanced venom apparatus. All are members of the family Viperidae. Their maxillary bone is very short, but deep, and able to move independently. The only teeth on these bones are the fangs, which are hollow tubes like hypodermic needles. There are two fang placements on each side, and in most cases the fangs are replaced about every two weeks. The fang placement that is not yet completely developed may still have a large enough fang so that at certain times three or four punctures may be inflicted by a single bite, although usually only one fang on each side is capable of penetrating in a given strike. When a viper's mouth is closed, its very long fangs are rotated on the maxillary bone back into the mouth against the upper jaw. When the snake strikes, the maxillary bone again rotates and the fangs are moved forward through an angle of 90 degrees to the biting position; then the venom gland muscle constricts as in proteroglyphs. Because the fangs are rotated to a position actually outside the confines of the mouth, a viperid snake may strike at an object of any size.

It has been suggested that solenoglyph vipers evolved from rear-fanged colubrids by progressively shortening the maxillary bone and reducing the number of teeth until the maxillary became so short that the only teeth left (the former rear fangs) were moved to the front.

All snakes have some type of teeth in varying sizes and numbers, but in most species there are backwardly curved, uniform teeth attached to the inside of the jaw, rather than in sockets. There are teeth on the premaxillary and maxillary bones of the upper jaw and the dentary bone of the lower jaw in most snakes. Many snakes have teeth on the palatine and pterygoid bones of the roof of the mouth as well. The replacement of teeth is continuous and steady during the life of most snakes, a condition known as polyphyodont. Replacement teeth grow in a fold of the mouth lining called the vagina dentis, and replacement of old teeth occurs in a regular pattern. Among the more bizarre adaptations of snakes are the esophageal teeth of the egg-eating snakes (*Dasypeltis scabra* and *Elaphe climacophora*) which function to break the shells of eggs so the contents can be eaten. These are not really teeth, but are projections of the vertebrae which protrude into the alimentary canal. The shells are not eaten by egg-eating snakes; they are regurgitated after their contents have been drained.

JACOBSON'S ORGAN

For some years now, scientists have understood the powers of the Jacobson's organ—that unique olfactory mechanism found in snakes. A snake's constantly flicking tongue is, in effect, smelling the air about it, picking up molecules of odor which it brings to a pair of sacs located on the roof of its mouth. These sacs, which are connected to the snake's olfactory nerve, "read" the molecules and transmit the information to the brain. Far more than sight and sound (a snake's sight and hearing are poorly developed), odor stimuli sensed through the Jacobson's organ control the behavior of snakes. This has been known for many years. But not until recently has work been done to determine just how a snake makes use of the information received through the Jacobson's organ. Must a snake learn through its environment which odors indicate food and which indicate danger, or is the skill innate, bred in over eons of evolution? The answer, or at least the beginnings of an answer, was supplied by Gordon M. Burghardt.

CHEMICAL PERCEPTION

Dr. Burghardt was primarily interested in how any living organism manages to sort out the chaos of stimuli—sights, sounds, smells, etc.—that its senses perceive. How does a creature separate from a riot of perceptions those indicating food or danger which are most

The long, forked tongue of a snake collects molecules from the air or ground and carries them inside the mouth, where the Jacobson's organ evaluates the taste and smell that the tongue picked up.

The grass snake (*Natrix natrix*) shown doing this is the most common of the harmless snakes found in England. It lays from 30 to 40 eggs, preferring a site where decaying organic matter, such as compost heaps, hay, and dung piles, maintains a more or less constant temperature. (*Photo: Photo-library Inc.*)

significant to it? Certainly in man much of the brain's selective ability is learned through experience, the way a mother learns to recognize her own child's cry in a room full of children, or a chef to recognize the absence of a particular spice in a complex dish. But, he reasoned, much of picking and choosing among stimuli is not conditioned by experience; rather, it is bred into an organism through evolution. Somehow a particular stimulus, which ethologists have come to call the *releaser* mechanism, will cause a particular organism to respond in a particular way, even if the organism has never experienced that stimulus before. Working with newborn snakes, removed from their natural environment, Burghardt was able to demonstrate that the food-attack response in snakes works just this way, and that the stimulus which releases the food-attack response is a particular odor of the food as perceived by the Jacobson's organ. Thus, evolution has bred into snakes a perceptual structure which ensures their ability to feed—and thus their survival—from the moment they are born.

Burghardt began his experiments by going back to the experiments conducted by Wilde in 1938. Wilde had been able to demonstrate that the attack mechanism in garter snakes is wholly dependent upon the Jacobson's organ. He made a clear, colorless solution of earthworm mucus, and presented it to the snakes on cotton swabs. Then he severed various nerves and was able to show that the snakes would attack the cotton swab no matter which sensory nerve was cut, as long as the nerve controlling the Jacobson's organ was intact. By repeating the experiment with newborn instead of adult snakes, Burghardt was able to demonstrate that the attack mechanism did not have to be learned; but rather was present when the snakes were born.

He began with a litter of three-day-old garter snakes which had never before been fed. He made solutions of various materials (red worms, minnows, mealworms, and horsemeat) by placing them in warm water for one minute, then offering the solutions to the snakes on cotton swabs. Red worms and minnows were natural food for the particular species; mealworms and horsemeat were not. He judged the attack mechanism to have been activated when the snake increased its tongue-flicking and then struck at the swab with open jaws. The snakes constantly attacked the red worm and minnow swabs, and did not attack the mealworm and horsemeat ones. Moreover, although they would not eat horsemeat, they attacked and ate pieces of horsemeat that had been dipped in the worm extract. At five-minute intervals a test series of twenty trials and then of forty was run, and the response of the snakes continued at the same strength, showing that the response mechanism could not be easily conditioned out. Having shown that the response was innate, specific, and fairly permanent, Burghardt then was able to carry his experimentation further.

By closing the snakes' eyes and then the nostrils (and then both together), he was able to show that the attack response was totally independent of both vision and the olfactory power unrelated to the Jacobson's organ. Furthermore, by carrying out similar tests with other species, which have different natural feeding habits than the garter snake, he was able to demonstrate that in each case the newborn snakes responded specifically to the stimuli representing foods normally eaten by these snakes in nature. The Chicago land garter snake (*Thamnophis sirtalis semifasciatus*) responded to swabs of fish, worms, amphibians, and leeches (its natural food) and not to slugs, mice, insects, and crayfish, which it does not normally eat. Both larval and adult salamanders were tested; the larval form brought on the attack response, whereas the adult form did not. In nature the snake will often eat the larval form and not the adult form. Apparently some chemical change takes place in the skin of the salamander as it changes, and this change determines its susceptibility to snake attack.

An oviparous species was also tested—the western smooth green snake (*Opheodrys vernalis blanchardi*)—with the same extracts that had been used in a series of garter snake tests. Only the swab dipped in cricket extract was attacked, and it was already known that the green snake eats only crickets among all the different foods tested.

When Burghardt tested water snakes, he found that two species, Graham's crayfish snake (*Regina grahami*) and the queen snake (*R. septemvittata*), which in nature eat nothing but crayfish, responded readily to crayfish extract, and not to the others offered, while other water snakes would respond to the extracts from fish and amphibians, which are among their natural prey.

However, the results of some experiments tended in another direction. For example, the aquatic garter snake responded readily to a swab dipped in guppy extract, yet guppies are seldom found in the snake's natural habitat. Furthermore, Butler's garter snake (*Thamnophis butleri*), which is known to subsist on worms and leeches in the field, responded readily and in captivity fed contentedly on fish and amphibians as well. Burghardt explains these exceptions in this way: "The normal feeding habits and ecology of a species are not 'sufficient' to explain the response to chemical cues in new-born young. But we should remember that evolution is a process of time and that the past may exist in the present. A feasible hypothesis is that Butler's garter snake . . . has retained the perceptual side of a releasing mechanism which appears to be of no selective advantage in its present mode of life. Of course, retention of the potential of native snakes to respond to chemical cues from fish would be advantageous if a change in the environment occurred so that fish became a necessary or more easily obtainable food source."

Finally, Burghardt tried experiments designed to test the power of the species-specific response over time. Half a litter of snakes was tested on the extracts for the first week of life, then released. The second half was raised from the start on strained liver which was force-fed. After periods of time (64 days in one case, 191 days in another), both groups were retested. The response to the specific swabs by the liver-fed snakes was just as strong as the response by the snakes raised on their natural food. The response was not only specific and innate; it would furthermore not degenerate even under the least natural of conditions.

GROWTH

Most people reflecting on the giant snakes—the boas, pythons, and anacondas—would associate them with generally tropical climates. Indeed, the world's largest snakes are inhabitants of the warmer regions of the world, and the largest snake in the United States, the 8½-foot indigo snake, is a midget by comparison. Two factors would seem to account for the large size attained by snakes in the tropics—the constant supply of food and the lack of cold temperatures. The latter, however, does not really account for the absolute size of a species, as it affects growth rate rather than maximum ultimate size. In areas that are cold, or areas that get colder than 70 degrees at any time during the year, snakes will hibernate for various lengths of time. The typical snake in the United States hibernates for half the year; thus it cannot be expected to eat as much or grow and mature as fast as a snake living in a warmer climate. This is not a hard-and-fast rule with respect to maximum size attained, even within a species, however. Many kingsnakes attain a larger size in the northern portions of their ranges than in the South. Another factor worth considering is that a snake as big as a python would be hard-pressed to find a burrow or sheltered area large enough for it to hibernate in. This could effectively preclude their distribution in cooler areas. However, Indian rock pythons hibernate briefly in northern India and Pakistan.

Largest of the rattlesnakes found in the Americas, this eastern diamond-back (*Crotalus adamanteus*), killed at Merritt Island, Florida, measured 80 inches without its rattle. The record size is 96 inches. (*Photo: NASA*)

Change with Growth

In general, young snakes very closely resemble their parents. Among venomous snakes, such as baby rattlesnakes and cobras, there are differences which are not obvious. In many of the venomous species, the venom is much more potent in the young to compensate for their small venom capacities. Young snakes often have brighter colors than the adult of the species, but in some cases they have entirely different color patterns. The black rat snake (*Elaphe obso-*

The black rat snake (*Elaphe obsoleta obsoleta*) is a large shiny snake that reaches a length of over 6 feet. Roger Conant authenticated a record-size specimen of 101 inches.

They are also known as "pilot" or mountain black snakes, sometimes retaining the traces of a spotted pattern that is pronounced when young. Randy Stechert caught a brown specimen of this species near Bear Mountain, New York. (*Photo: Roy Pinney*) *leta obsoleta*) is one of our best-known rat snakes. Its young look like the adult of the blotched rat snake in color pattern, however. So do the young of the yellow rat snake (*E. obsoleta quadrivittata*). Among many genera of snakes that have been well studied, other ontogenetic differences are apparent, although not as obvious. The head, eye, and tail are proportionally larger with respect to the rest of the body in all young kingsnakes and rat snakes than in adults. The number and distribution of scales is constant from birth to adulthood in all known snakes.

TEMPERATURE

Snakes are commonly referred to as being cold-blooded, although it has been demonstrated that some pythons can in fact increase their body temperature metabolically to some extent. Other snakes can control their body temperatures by various behavioral responses to heat or cold. A better word to refer to the body temperature of snakes is "poikilothermic," which means that the temperature fluctuates with that of the environment. The basic reason snakes cannot maintain a high body temperature is that their metabolic rate is only about one tenth that of mammals, and consequently their bodies produce much less internal heat. Because of the poikilothermic condition, snakes depend on their environmental temperature for almost all aspects of their activity.

All snakes have certain critical temperature ranges which control their activities. Those can be wide or narrow, and may differ considerably from one species to another. All snakes have a lethal maximum temperature; this is generally about 112 degrees. They have a lethal minimum temperature as well, which is just below freezing. Temperatures at either extreme make it imperative that the snake quickly do something to adjust to the temperature, such as hibernate or find a cool place, lest they die. There is a hibernation range as well; this is from 40 to 50 degrees down to the lethal minimum for most species. There is a resting range, which for most snakes is between the minimum temperature that will not induce hibernation and 70 or more degrees. At these temperatures, snakes will not eat, travel, or reproduce, but will remain "awake." The activity ranges of many snakes is very wide. Garter snakes can be active from 41 to 95 degrees, and are generally thought to have the lowest active temperature. Rat snakes have the highest active temperature, about 100 degrees.

The temperature of the air has the least affect on the temperature of a snake. Basking snakes pick up more heat from the substrates on which they lie than from the air. Many snakes are found on asphalt roads at night because these roads absorb much heat and retain it longer than the surrounding ground, thus affording the snake a substrate which will keep it warm.

SALT GLANDS

Animals which live in the sea are faced with the problem of maintaining their normal physiological salt balance. This is so because life arose in the seas, perhaps over a billion years ago, at a time

A northern blacktail rattlesnake (*Crotalus molossus molossus*), clearly showing the heat-sensitive pit organ. (*Photo: M. V. Rubio*)

when the salt content of the water was lower than it is now. Since that period, much salt has dissolved from the land into the seas. Because the salt balance inside the cells of sea snakes matches that of the ancient seas in which life evolved, when they returned to the modern ocean they found it too salty for them. Consequently, at least in the genus *Laticauda,* a natrial gland in the palate of the mouth has evolved which serves to eliminate excess salt. A thirsty person cannot benefit from drinking salt water because elimination of excess salt requires more fresh water than was consumed.

PIT ORGANS

Heat-sensitive pit organs are present in the snakes of the subfamily Crotalinae (rattlesnakes, copperheads, cottonmouths, and their relatives) and also in many boas and pythons.

Labial pits are very noticeable on this reticulated python (*Python reticulatus*) although many boids do not have them. These sensitive heat detectors have been found capable of accurately measuring thermal variations to within .001 degrees centigrade and are used to aid in hunting warm-blooded prey after dark.

Scientists are eager to learn how they operate, since they are more directional and selective than anything ever built by man. (*Photo: Roy Pinney*)

The heat-sensitive organ in pit vipers is on the head between the nostril and eye, almost directly above the insertion of each functional fang. They are noticeable depressions with an outer and inner chamber innervated by the trigeminal nerve. The organs constantly respond to the amount of radiant heat reaching them, and are most sensitive to the infrared. Sudden changes in heat radiating from objects in the receptive field of the snake's pit caused the most marked responses. Nerve impulses transmitted from the pit organ depend on the temperature of contrasting objects in the environment and are not at all dependent on the temperature of the snake. Consequently, an object colder than the rest of the environment being scanned by the pit will cause a reduction in pit activity, regardless of the body temperature of the snake. Pit vipers can detect a change of temperature of a fraction of a degree centrigrade. The pit organ is most important in food capture at night, as the pit will allow a snake to detect a passing rodent in total darkness.

The labial scales of certain boid snakes possess pits which are also heat-sensitive. However, there are other boids which do not have pits but seem to be heat-sensitive. The pits increase the directional sensitivity to heat. The patterns of pit distribution are different in boas and pythons. Among the boids possessing well-developed pits are the American rosy boa (*Lichanura trivirgata*).

LUNGS

Like birds and mammals, snakes breathe entirely by their lungs, which are much more compartmentalized than those of amphibians, but considerably less complex than those of mammals. Because of their elongate body form, snakes show various degrees of reduction in the size of the left lung. In boids, the left lung may be nearly as large as the right. This represents the most primitive condition. In the typhlopoids and colubroids, the left lung is vestigial or absent. In the blind snake family Typhlopidae there are snakes with a tracheal lung. The trachea may or may not divide into two bronchi in other snakes depending on whether the left lung is reduced or totally absent.

GLANDS

Very little is known about the endocrine system in snakes. They do possess standard endocrine glands, such as the thyroid, parathyroids, adrenals, pituitary, and islets of Langerhans in the pancreas. The adrenal glands of snakes which eat toads, such as the hognose snake (genus *Heterodon*), are very large, and are thought to play a role in protecting the snake from toad venoms.

The western hognose snake (*Heterodon nasicus*), like most of the other hognose snakes, eats toads as its principal food and is not affected by that amphibian's toxic secretions. (*Photo: Los Angeles Zoo/Sy Oskeroff*)

KIDNEYS

Snakes have paired metanephric kidneys, with the right one being anterior to the left. In some snakes, the posterior convoluted tubules within the kidney nephrons (filtering units) are swollen in males and apparently secrete a fluid in which the sperm are ultimately suspended. The primary excretory product of snakes is the semisolid uric acid. By excreting uric acid, snakes are able to conserve water and inhabit arid environments.

LIVER

All snakes have a liver, and this organ is unspectacular in the boids and colubroids, but in the blind snakes (typhlopoids) it is composed of 11 to 27 lobes.

Snake Behavior

ENEMIES AND DEFENSE

Snakes, like all living creatures, have their quota of persistent enemies—including other snakes, such as the krait and the king cobra, although some are protected by immunity against their venom. More often, however, it is the predator who has this factor on its side. The kingsnake and the tropical American mussurana, with high or complete resistance to the venom of pit vipers, can devour with impunity the fer-de-lance, rattlesnakes, cottonmouths, and copperheads.

Some mammals, notably the Asiatic mongoose (*Herpestes edwardii*), have a high level of tolerance for the venom of the Indian cobra, as well as being adept at dodging its strike. The meerkat (*Suricata*) of South Africa, while susceptible to the bite of puff adders, apparently resists that of the Cape cobra. Certain hedgehogs are virtually immune to adder venom, and some opossums and skunks are safe from pit vipers. The great majority of mammals on the long list of enemies, including dogs, pigs, badgers, and foxes, have no such physiological defenses. Nor do birds, such as the golden eagle, buzzards, owls, secretary birds, and roadrunners, yet they have always exacted their toll as inveterate enemies of snakes.

Man, however, frequently and with justification called the most dangerous of all animals, is the snake's most deadly opponent, even as he is his own. There are times and places in which he seems dedicated to almost total war against venomous and nonvenomous species alike. Ignorance, blind fear, and in most instances a combination of both, impel him to what amounts to senseless slaughter, not only with club or gun but even with the tires of his vehicles. All

Man is a prime enemy of snakes, but there are many others among the mammals, birds, and reptiles (including snakes). Photo shows a common snapping turtle (*Chelydra serpentina*), one of the most abundant turtles in the United States, with a snake in its steel-trap jaws. (*Photo: Pinney/Chase*)

too often the driver through rural areas, perhaps imbued with the smug and naïve notion that he is performing a public service, sights a snake crossing the highway and swerves to flatten it. "D.O.R.'s" are all too common a sight on the road, killed by speeding automobiles.

But these individual-kill "hit men" are by no means alone. Altogether too many amateur collectors, who most certainly should know better, are overzealous and shortsighted in bagging many more specimens than they can have reasonable use for—specimens which soon wind up dead.

Most regrettable of all, however, are the wholesale depredations committed by or resulting from invasions of the natural environment of snakes as a result of industrial and agricultural expansion. The purely commercial hunter, who is committed to financial gain and presumably overlooks the end result of exterminating a species, is likewise an enemy on a wholesale scale. The snake obviously cannot, either literally or figuratively, strike back. But when it comes to the natural, individual enemy, and the balance of ecology is not disturbed in his disfavor, he has many ways and means of self-protection.

Some of the behavioral adaptations that various snakes have acquired for their protection include the following defense mechanisms:

CONCEALING COLORATION

The vine snake (*Oxybelis aeneus*) is a very thin, attenuate green serpent which lives in tropical vegetation. Hanging motionless from a tree, it indeed would be very hard to distinguish from a vine. The coloration and body shape which conceal it from its enemies also deceive the lizards upon which it feeds. The North American smooth green snake (*Opheodrys vernalis*) is also green and very thin but it lives in green grass, rather than in trees, and is likewise very well camouflaged. Both of these stalking bright green snakes are quite striking when photographed against white or black backgrounds.

Among the African vipers of the genus *Bitis* are some of the thickest and most spectacularly colored and most venomous snakes in the world. The very large (up to 7 feet in length) Gaboon viper (*B. gabonica*) is certainly one of the most sought-after display snakes for zoos because of its complex color pattern of bright blue, tan, and black. On the forest floor, however, this pattern serves to disrupt the outline of the body and helps conceal this large snake. The even more vividly colored, although slightly smaller rhinoceros viper (*B. nasicornis*) is yellow and blue, blotched with lateral triangles of dark color on a background of pink, purple, or green. Its pattern blends well with the forest floor. The faded gray or buff-colored

The rough green snake (*Opheodrys aestivus*) ranges from Connecticut to Florida, is mild-tempered and arboreal. The scales are prominently keeled.

The eastern smooth green snake (*O. vernalis*) does not have keeled scales and is less arboreal than the rough green snake. Its prime diet is insects, spiders, and an occasional frog. Insecticides seemingly have reduced its numbers in the northeastern United States. (*Photo: Roy Pinney*)

horned puff adder (*B. caudalis*) matches the color of the sand that it lives on.

There are hundreds of less striking examples of cryptic coloration in snakes, and in fact many species native to the United States are most often caught on roads at night because they are almost impossible to spot against their natural backgrounds during the day.

The Gaboon viper (*Bitis gabonica gabonica*), encountered in the tropical rain forests of Africa, including Zululand, can develop the longest venom-discharging fangs—up to two inches in length in large specimens —which can penetrate deep into the flesh of a victim to produce rapid and effectively lethal results. FitzSimons notes that while the hemolytic element predominates in other vipers and the venom is mainly neurotoxic in cobras, the Gaboon viper carries both blood and nerve toxins, together with other dangerous elements of an extremely high potency, causing death within a short time unless the most effective, and preferably specific, antivenin measures are taken immediately. (*Photo: SATOUR*)

WARNING COLORATION

Many venomous snakes have, rather than concealing color patterns, aposematic or warning colors, which apparently advertise the danger of their presence. The exact effectiveness of warning coloration is uncertain, as many predators (notably mammals) are color-blind. However, primates and birds can see color and theoretically should be able to associate the bright color patterns with danger. Among the most spectacular of the warning-colored snakes are the coral snakes, venomous elapids with bands of alternating red and black or red, yellow, and black encircling their bodies. They occur in many parts of the world, including Africa (*Aspidelaps*), Southeast Asia (*Calliophis* and *Maticora*), Australia (*Brachyurophis*), and the Americas (genera *Micrurus* and *Micruroides*). *Micruroides*

The eastern coral snake (*Micrurus fulvius fulvius*) is usually 20–30 inches in length when adult. They are found in Florida north to North Carolina and west to Mississippi and Louisiana. A small mouth and short fangs make it difficult for them to bite some parts of the human body, but fingers and toes are vulnerable and their venom is potent. Their diet includes snakes, lizards, and frogs. (*Photo: Roy Pinney*)

consists of a single species, the Arizona coral snake, which has broad bands of red, yellow, and black with the red and yellow touching. Likewise, the representatives of *Micrurus* in the United States, the eastern and Texas coral snakes, have the tricolor pattern. As one goes south of the United States, where there are over forty-five species of *Micrurus,* the patterns become more complicated. In South America there are numerous tricolor triad species which have three black bands separated by two yellow bands, the entire black triad surrounded by red bands. Among the tricolor triad coral snakes are the southern coral snake (*M. frontalis*), the Surinam coral snake (*M. surinamensis*), and the Amazon coral snake (*M. spixii*). The last-named is a giant coral snake of over 4 feet in length and is extremely dangerous.

Russell's viper (*Vipera russelii*), a brightly colored viperid snake of India and Southeast Asia, is one of the world's major causes of snakebite deaths.

MIMICRY

Two entirely different types of mimetic coloration are common in snakes: mimicry of the head by the tail and mimicking dangerous species in overall coloration.

Tail mimicry is seen in both harmless and venomous snakes and is an attempt to divert the attention of predators from the head by waving a brightly colored (usually red) tail underside, which looks like a head poised to strike. Two common North American snakes engage in tail displays. These are the ringneck snakes (*Diadophis*) and the mud snake (*Farancia abacura*). Both have red tail undersides, and the mud snake has, in addition, a stubbly tail with a small spine at its end. The overall effect is that of a head with a stinger or horn. Interestingly enough, many of the coral snakes (including species of *Calliophis* and *Maticora*) also engage in tail displays, as they are reluctant biters.

The Arizona coral snake is mimicked by a number of harmless snakes, including the Arizona mountain kingsnake (*Lampropeltis pyromelana*). The organ pipe shovelnose snake (*Chionactis palarostris organica*) is another Arizona coral snake mimic, and although its yellow bands are not as wide as those of the coral snake, they do touch the red bands as in the venomous model. The eastern coral

The northern ringneck snake (*Diadophis punctatus edwardsi*) has a yellow collar and belly in sharp contrast to its otherwise drab dark brown-black-gray coloration. When newborn they are about 4 inches long and have keeled scales which disappear as they mature into adults about 12 inches long. (*Photo: Roy Pinney*)

snake (*Micrurus fulvius*) has a number of good mimics with red, yellow, and black bands, including the scarlet snake (*Cemophora coccinea*) and a number of forms of the milk snake (*Lampropeltis triangulum*). The milk snake offers good support for the mimicry hypothesis in that it does not mimic the coral snake's pattern in areas where the coral snake is not found. In the eastern United States, the drab milk snake becomes the scarlet kingsnake (*L. triangulum elapsoides*), another excellent coral snake mimic but again one whose red and yellow bands do not touch. Another milk snake subspecies, the Mexican milk snake of Mexico and southern Texas, also mimics the coral snake. Such mimics as are listed above are called Batesian mimics; they are harmless snakes which resemble a venomous one. The mimics must be less common than their model, else their patterns will be associated with palatability by predators.

In Central and South America, coral snakes are simulated by rear-fanged colubrids as well. Such mimicry of one venomous snake by another (in this case a more venomous one by a less venomous one) is called Mullerian mimicry. It is hypothesized that Mullerian mimics reinforce each other's message of danger to those that see them; therefore there are no true models and mimics, and all species may be plentiful in number. Among the best Mullerian mimics of coral snakes in these regions are the Aesculapian snakes of the genus *Erythrolamprus,* moderately venomous rear-fanged snakes which may even mimic the triad color arrangements of coral snakes. The fact that island forms of the Aesculapian snake (which have no coral snakes on their islands) are cryptically colored rather than tricolor helps reinforce the mimicry hypothesis, which is still not accepted by all authorities.

DIVERSION TACTICS

When threatened, many snakes exhibit unusual behaviors which may startle or disgust a potential predator. The American hognose snake (*Heterodon*) acts in a way which may totally confuse even a human. If it is threatened and cannot escape, it flattens its head into a hood not unlike a cobra, hisses loudly, and strikes repeatedly at the attacker with its mouth closed! If this fails to dissuade the attacker, the hognose snake will go through mock convulsions, lose

The acts of the hognose snake (*Heterodon platyrhinos*), the clown of the snake world, have to be seen to be believed. When provoked it spreads the rear of the head and neck to create the effect of a hooded angry cobra, then inhales to blow itself up, exhales so as to emit a long pronounced hiss, and if such a performance doesn't seem to work, it simply turns over on its back, the body becoming limp, the mouth open with tongue hanging out, shudders convulsively a couple of times, and appears to have died from a heart attack. Flip it over on its belly and it will immediately twist around on its back. When all seems to be safe, the snake will turn on its belly and glide away. The snake in the photograph is the black phase. The diet is largely toads. (*Photo: M. V. Rubio*)

its muscle tone, and flip over on its back with its tongue hanging out. If it is turned right side up, it will flip over and play dead again. Such behavior is often sufficient to scare off or confuse an intruder. Curiously, the hognose snake, which is mildly venomous, never seems to bite when threatened.

Many snakes when bothered secrete foul-smelling muck from their glands near the cloaca. Such "stinking" behavior often dissuades attackers.

Two American boas, the rosy boa (*Lichanura trivirgata*) and the rubber boa (*Charina bottae*), employ the "balling" defense mechanism. When bothered, they roll up into a ball. The rosy boa has a blunt tail, which it often leaves protruding from the coiled ball to act as a false head while its real head remains hidden within the coils. The rosy boa is even known to strike with its tail while coiled.

DISPLAY INTIMIDATION

Some snakes display intimidation behavior which is either unusual or impressive. The king cobra is known to elevate its anterior portion as much as four feet off the ground and emit a sound similar to a dog's growl.

A 14-foot king cobra (*Ophiophagus hannah*) raises its head at the approach of the photographer. The maximum length recorded is about 18 feet. Also called the hamadryad, it feeds mainly on snakes. (*Photo: Charlotte Bourdier/Haast*)

The taipan (*Oxyuranus scutellatus*), whose powerful venom can result in the death of a human being in a few minutes, flattens its head when cornered and compresses its neck vertically. The body is expanded so that the skin between the scales is visible, and is coiled into a series of loops and partially raised off the ground as the tail waves back and forth. The strike of the taipan is noted for its speed. If its intimidation posturing does not work, it may strike several times before the intruder can even move. Fortunately, the taipan is rare and found only in northeastern Australia.

MOUTH GAPING

Open-mouth displays are used in the threat or bluff postures of a variety of snakes and by other reptiles, mammals, and birds. Certain snakes when threatened or cornered will open their mouths to display the white inner lining. The significance of this behavior is not fully understood, but it is often seen in snakes which have no other white dorsal coloration and it may be that the sudden appearance of a contrasting color could startle would-be predators.

Two American snakes are well known for this behavior. The venomous cottonmouth moccasin (*Agkistrodon piscivorus*) derives its name from the fact that, when threatened, it may display the above-mentioned white mouth lining. This behavior is often accompanied by hissing. Another American snake which does this commonly is the rear-fanged vine snake (*Oxybelis aeneus*).

On a recent trip to Colima, Mexico, the author, accompanied by Robert Price, had an unusual encounter with a 3-foot, pencil-thin *Oxybelis*. We had hired a local guide to take us to the remote areas of Colima, not far from the active Volcán de Colima. Our guide, while entirely self-taught, was surprisingly well informed about venomous snakes and had an uncanny ability to locate them in thick foliage by sound as well as sight. He spotted the motionless vine snake in a thick patch of lianas and shrubs, and tried to call it to our attention, as he was somewhat hesitant about how to catch this rear-fanged snake, whose bite causes swelling and localized numbness. We might not have caught the vine snake at all had it not been for its mouth gaping. Price finally spotted the white mouth lining, the only part of the otherwise brown animal which contrasted with the underbrush. He deftly grabbed at the snake's head from behind, just as the animal coiled to strike. As I readied a snake bag to receive the serpent, Price extricated the snake and, to our surprise, the befuddled vine snake had bitten itself squarely in the neck while being captured!

HOODS

Hoods or other expanding structures in the neck regions of snakes can exaggerate their size and thus help ward off predators. The dangerous rear-fanged African bird snake (*Thelotornis kirtlandii*) is a slender, pointy-headed tree dweller which when annoyed inflates its neck greatly. The pointed head atop a wide round neck looks much like a small bird, hence the snake's common name. False rat snakes of the genus *Gonyosoma* also have a large inflatable neck pouch.

Undoubtedly the most famous hooded snakes are the cobras and their allies. These snakes spread their hoods by means of movable ribs in their necks. All of the true cobras (genus *Naja*) have hoods, as do the spitting cobra (*Hemachatus*) and the king cobra (*Ophiophagus hannah*). The water cobras (genus *Boulengerina*) have narrow hoods, as do the tree cobras (*Pseudohaje*). The Australian black and mulga snakes (*Pseudechis*) are capable of flattening their necks into a slight hoodlike expansion when annoyed. Although hooded snakes may look more formidable to most predators, the Indian mongoose commonly kills and eats cobras.

Recently, herpetologists working with the bird snake have evolved a new theory about its throat expansion. They assert that, when mobbed by sunbirds, the bird snake inflates its neck so that it looks like a fledgling in a begging posture. The stretched skin and contrasting scales of the snake's throat resemble the sunbird's breast plumage, further compounding the illusion. It is possible that bird snakes lure unwary sunbirds in this fashion.

CONSTRICTION

The art of prey constriction was perfected by the boid snakes long before the evolution of venom by viperids and elapids. Large constrictors existed in the Eocene Epoch over 40 million years ago. Constriction subsequently evolved in a substantial number of colubrid snakes, including the kingsnakes and rat snakes.

Constricting snakes attempt to seize their prey by the head, thus reducing the chance of the snake's being injured by the jaws of its victim. A number of body coils are then thrown around the prey. As the animal exhales, the coils are tightened and the prey is prevented from breathing. Seldom do constrictors actually crush or internally injure their victims. The combination of constriction and envenomation has evolved in some rear-fanged colubrids such as *Madagascarophis*. There is evidence to indicate that, when constricting, boid snakes face their own bellies, whereas colubrids face their dorsal surfaces, but this has not been authenticated for a great many species.

ARBOREALS

Many reptiles live in trees and bushes and have slight modifications that enable them to go from branch to branch. Arboreal members of the colubrid family such as the mambas and vine snakes have elongated bodies, while boas, pythons, and vipers have short,

The beaked snake (*Rhamphiophis oxyrhynchus rostratus*) is found in South Africa, southern Sudan, Abyssinia, Kenya, and Mozambique, particularly in sandy thorn or bushveld country, where it is often found in gerbil burrows or in the terminal chambers of termite hills. Its diet appears to be restricted to prey of small size such as insects, lizards, frogs, other snakes, and small mammals. (*Photo: John Pitts/SATOUR*)

prehensile tails, which can be wrapped around a limb as a safety measure against falling. Other snakes are excellent climbers, ascending vertically on trees by flexing the muscles of the skin so that the scales achieve a "foothold" on the bark and branches. Most of the tropical forms have large heads, prominent eyes, and pointed snouts. Their coloration blends with the leaves and when motionless are difficult to spot at a short distance.

The green mamba (*Dendroaspis angusticeps*) is one of the four species of mambas currently recognized. They range over most of central and southern Africa, and because of their size, speed, and highly toxic venom, they are considered among the most dangerous of all snakes.

The green mamba is mostly arboreal, is shy, and avoids man if possible. Its venom is about half as toxic as that of the more dangerous black mamba. (*Photo: Roy Pinney*)

Sand boas (*Eryx sp.*) range from North and East Africa to India
and central Asia. They live beneath the surface of the soil, especially in
sandy regions, where they "swim" through the sand feeding on equally
subterranean lizards. In contrast to other boas living in the treetops or in
the rivers, their body is characteristically adjusted to burrowing, as that
of the tree snakes is to arboreal life. The head is shortened and the tail,
at a quick glance, looks like the head. (*Photo: Roy Pinney*)

BURROWING

Burrowing is a way of life for many snakes, limbless lizards, and tortoises. A sharp, pointed snout attached to a strong, rigid skull makes a good tool for shoveling through the ground. It's an adaptation for underground living seen in many burrowing animals. Snakes best adapted for this kind of existence are generally small in size, short in the tail, and small in the head with very small eyes. The head is forced into the sand, mud, or soil with the rostral shield, which is frequently thickened and comparatively large.

The Pima leafnose snake (*Phyllorhynchus browni browni*), about a foot long, found in the southwestern United States, is a desert species about which little is known. When annoyed, they coil like rattlesnakes and strike but their bite is not venomous. The scale at the tip of the snout is used as a burrowing aid to avoid the heat of the sun. (*Photo: M. V. Rubio*)

SPITTING COBRAS

Most venomous snakes use their hollow, needlelike fangs to inject venom into an animal or intruder. Two African cobras and an Asian cobra have fangs which are even further modified to spray venom at the eyes of an intruder up to ten feet away. The spitter's fangs have reduced openings which are directed toward the front rather than downward. As the muscles surrounding the venom glands eject the venom through the hollow fangs, the animal exhales strongly. The exhalation converts the stream of venom to clouds of droplets. Venom in the eyes is very painful and can cause temporary blindness.

The spitting cobra (*Naja nigricollis*), averaging 5 to 6 feet, is found in Africa south of the Sahara. Although it seldom bites, it can "spit," actually squirt, like a water pistol under considerable pressure, up to nine feet. If the venom contacts the eyes it causes great pain and spasm of the eyelids, with subsequent eye-tissue damage unless the venom is washed out immediately with water or some other nonirritating liquid. (*Photo: Roy Pinney*)

LOCOMOTION

Snakes have no limbs but they have evolved different ways of moving about with considerable efficiency.

Rectilinear motion is accomplished by muscle connections between the ribs and a ventral surface. Two important sets of muscles are involved, the inferior and superior costo-cutaneous. The superior muscles contract and elevate successive patches of belly scales which are then planted against the substrate. Contraction of the inferior muscles pulls the rest of the body forward over the firmly planted, but loosely attached belly scales. This pattern spreads down the body, and as a result the snake moves forward in a straight line. This type of motion is most often employed by large, heavy-bodied snakes such as boas, pythons, and the Gaboon viper.

Serpentine motion, in which a snake throws its body into a series of lateral sine waves, depends largely on friction with the ground. The propulsion needed for this type of movement is derived from the push-off of each curve against the substrate. If the substrate is

The sidewinder (*Crotalus cerastes cerastes*) weaves its natural way of progression across the desert sands. Essentially, sidewinding involves a side-flowing or looping motion whereby only vertical forces are applied to the supporting surface. (*Photo: Walt Disney Productions*)

very flat, serpentine motion is ineffective. Nearly all snakes use serpentine motion at one time or another. This type of motion is used by tree snakes and is also employed by snakes when swimming.

Many snakes which live in areas with smooth substrates and those snakes which travel through narrow passages employ concertina motion. In this case, the snake draws up the stationary part of its body into closely spaced sine curves and extends its anterior portion straight forward and then the process is repeated. A very unusual tree snake (*Chrysopelea ornata*) uses this method to climb vertically up trees. It possesses keeled ventral scales which it can brace against the tree bark for support while thrusting its anterior portion upward.

Finally, desert species often rely on what is thought to be the most efficient method of snake locomotion over smooth surfaces, sidewinding. Sidewinding is a complicated process whose specifics are very difficult to explain. A sidewinding snake raises its head and anterior section slightly off the surface and throws them sideways at about a right angle to the rest of the extended body. The head rests on the ground in the new position and the anterior body spans the

The racers (*Coluber sp.*) and coachwhips (*Masticophis sp.*) have slender forms well suited to skimming over the ground at great speed.

The striped racer (*Masticophis lateralis*), found in the Southwest, is about 5 feet long when adult. (*Photo: M. V. Rubio*)

old and new positions, slightly elevated off the substrate. The snake then lifts the posterior portion of its body section over to new line of contact, keeping at least two areas of its body in surface contact. A new series is started before the first one is completed. The net result is that the head of the snake moves at an angle of over 90 degrees to the left or right of the longitudinal body axis.

Some snakes, such as the black racer and the coachwhips, appear to move very rapidly. When timed, however, it has been found that the fastest of snakes can move at only about 5 miles per hour and then only for very brief spurts. The illusion of great speed probably results from the long slender form of the animal. As its body pours into the crack in an old stone wall, or is lost to sight in the dappled interior of a brush pile, the human observer imagines that the snake moves much faster than it actually does.

AUDIBLE WARNINGS

Audible warnings, other than the rattle devices of *Crotalus* and related genera, are noted in the bushmaster, moccasin, copperhead, and a few other species which may vibrate their tails very rapidly to produce a staccato tattoo. The saw-scaled viper (*Echis carinatus*), asps (*Cerastes*), and egg-eating snakes (*Dasypeltis*) are among the snakes that practice a form of stridulation by rubbing together their jagged scales to make a grating sound.

The tiny western hooknose snake (*Gyalopion canum*) has one of the most bizarre diversion tactics of all. When annoyed, it will make believe it is severely injured and will writhe on the ground. While doing so, it extrudes and retracts the lining of its cloaca, the air making a popping sound.

HISSING

Hissing in snakes is a result of exhalation, and in snakes with large lungs, the hiss is noticeably louder. The bullsnakes (*Pituophis*) are unique in having an epiglottis which greatly magnifies the hiss by vibrating. If annoyed, gopher snakes and bullsnakes also assume a strike pose, vibrating the tail rapidly.

The Pacific gopher snake (*Pituophis melanoleucus catenifer*) averages between 4 and 5 feet in length when fully grown. Because of the enormous numbers of mice, pocket gophers, and other rodents which make up the bulk of its diet, it is regarded as economically important and accordingly protected. (*Photo: Roy Pinney*)

The saw-scaled viper (*Echis carinatus*) is a very deadly snake of East Africa, western Asia, India, and Ceylon, remarkable for having scales that produce a sharp rasping sound when the body coils are rubbed together. (*Photo: Roy Pinney*)

CRYING

The Indian rock python (*Python molurus molurus*), which inhabits burrows near the edge of water, dense clumps of vegetation, large rotten logs, caves, ruins, and slopes of marshy forests and nearby rocky ledges, has been observed when alarmed to make a loud hissing sound similar to that of a crying human baby.

CAUDAL LURING

A few snakes have developed morphological modifications which act as lures for potential prey animals. Baby copperheads (*Agkistrodon contortrix*) possess yellow tips on their tails which they wave back and forth to attract small frogs. Australian death adders

(*Acanthophis antarcticus*) use the tail to attract small mammals and birds within range of their lethal bite. Several rattlesnakes, including the southern Pacific rattlesnake (*Crotalus viridis helleri*), the rock rattlesnake (*C. lepidus*), and the pigmy rattlesnake (*Sistrurus miliarus*), also possess yellow tail lures as juveniles.

Ross Allen, the well-known snake collector, observed young cantils (*Agkistrodon bilineatus*) waving their yellow-tipped tails to attract frogs. The frogs attempted to eat the tail tips and were killed and eaten by the cantils.

The curious vine snake (*Oxybelis aeneus*) may employ a head-and-tongue lure to attract prey. It has been postulated that the tendency of this snake to sway gently from a tree or vine with its mouth closed is an attempt to lure or fascinate potential prey animals. This theory has fallen out of favor somewhat in recent years, but E. D. Keiser, who did a detailed study of this animal, reported that in 112 instances lizards seemed to be fascinated by the thin, waving head of the vine snake.

TERRITORIALITY

Individual animals typically remain within a familiar area, their home range. Snakes, however, are not known to defend the territory in which they live, eat, mate, and hibernate. Several studies have been made of snakes marked and recaptured to determine how far their ranges extend. A black racer (*Coluber constrictor*) was found just over a mile from where it had been marked two years before. Garter snakes (*Thamnophis sirtalis*) traveled a mile and a half in 41 days. It would appear that long travels over a relatively short period of time may represent movement from or toward a hibernaculum which may be outside the normal home range of the active snake. It is thought that male snakes wander more than females, and juveniles have smaller home ranges than adults. Home ranges for copperheads (*Agkistrodon contortrix*) in Kansas average about 24.4 acres for males and 8.5 for females, according to one study. For black rat snakes (*Elaphe obsoleta*) the average home ranges are 29 acres for males and 24 for females, including the area where the snake is active, but excluding hibernacula which may be a considerable distance away.

Radio transmitters were force-fed to western diamondback rattle-

The copperhead (*Agkistrodon contortrix*) has several subspecies which often intergrade: southern (*A. c. contortrix*), broad-banded (*A. c. laticinctus*), northern (*A. c. mokeson*), Osage (*A. c. phaeogaster*), and Trans-Pecos (*A. c. pictigaster*).

Their diet has included seventeen-year locusts, mice, caterpillars, and shrews. While copperheads account for the great majority of snakebites seen in the eastern United States, fatalities are almost unknown. (*Photo: Roy Pinney*)

snakes (*Crotalus atrox*) that were released and followed in their natural habitat in southwestern Oklahoma by Hobart F. Landreth. Movements, behavior, and ecology of these snakes were studied for a two-year period.

The activity periods of *C. atrox* fluctuated seasonally as animals moved during midday (winter), early morning and late evening (spring and fall), and midnight (summer). Migrations to and from the dens occurred in spring and fall. The summer range was basically the same each year and extended 1–2 kilometers from the den. Rattlesnakes did not wander randomly but moved in directed courses. Results from orientation tests lead one to conclude that *C. atrox* can pick up solar clues and that they can use these to learn directional goals.

COURTSHIP AND MATING

The climax of courtship is copulation. Male snakes rely primarily upon vision and their sense of smell to locate females during the breeding season. Chemical perception of female scents by males is necessary for courtship and mating behavior. Once a male snake has located a female, the ensuing courtship depends largely on proper physical stimulation of the female and olfactory stimulation of the male. In most of the species in which mating behavior has been studied, the male which has successfully followed a female's scent,

Two black racers (*Coluber constrictor*) mating. Male snakes have not one but two penises, called hemipenes, each of which is connected to its own testis. How does an aroused snake decide which hemipenis to use? David Crews of the Harvard Museum of Comparative Zoology has found that some reptiles do not appear to favor one hemipenis over the other. If one is surgically removed, the reptile simply assumes a position best suited to insert the other hemipenis and transmit its spermatozoa to the female's cloaca. If one testis is removed leaving the hemipenis intact, the reptile tends to use the hemipenis still connected to a testis. The conclusion is that the sensory feedback from the testis is important in helping the reptile decide which hemipenis to use. (*Photo: Roy Pinney*)

or otherwise located her, will wave his tail back and forth signifying a readiness to mate. The male generally approaches from behind and rubs his chin over the female's body while flicking his tongue to pick up scents. The chin rubbing is thought to stimulate receptors in the chin scales of the male which ready him for copulation.

As most female snakes try to avoid males at first, the male often winds his tail around the female's so that he may secure himself on top of her and bring their cloacal regions close together. In many species of snakes, once the male has positioned himself properly, waves of muscle contractions pass from his tail to his head. These presumably stimulate the female. In other snakes the male may bite the female to excite her. In the rattlesnakes, the male jerks and twitches his body to stimulate the female. Male boas and pythons have small rudiments, where the hind legs of their ancestors were, with which they scratch the female's back. The ultimate result of these various kinds of stimulation is "permission" of the female for the male to insert one of his hemipenes. Copulation in snakes may last for several hours.

MALE COPULATORY ORGANS

All male squamates (snakes, lizards, and amphisbaenians) have two hollow copulatory organs called hemipenes. They are unique among all vertebrates in this respect. One hemipenis is located on each side of the base of the tail, and during copulation only one of them is everted. Eversion is achieved by a combination of increased blood flow and lymph pressure in the erectile walls of the organ, which have numerous sinuses, at least one pair for lymph and one pair for blood. Constrictor muscles keep the blood and lymph inside the organ. The organ is withdrawn by retractor muscles which pull from the inside, causing the organ to invert. The process of inversion can be likened to pressing your finger into the tip of a cylindrical balloon, causing the outside walls to move inside the depression created by the finger.

Each hemipenis has a sperm groove called a sulcus spermaticus, as well as a variety of "ornamentations." The latter may consist of spines, calyces (cuplike structures), flounces (folded strips), and papillae. The great herpetologist Edward Drinker Cope found that the overall appearance of the hemipenis is quite constant within a

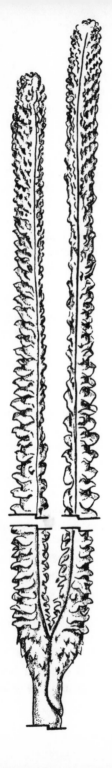

Every male snake possesses two copulatory organs called hemipenes. Either the left or the right organ is used in any given copulation. The size and ornamentation of the hemipenes are species-specific, although in rare cases a very closely related species may gain entry into the cloaca of a female. The diversity of snake hemipenes presents a formidable barrier against hybridization and helps maintain the integrity of the species in situations where interbreeding might otherwise occur.

The hemipenis of the king cobra (*Ophiophagus hannah*), shown here, is the largest reptilian copulatory organ. It may exceed 18 inches in length when fully everted. (*Drawings courtesy of H. G. Dowling*) species, and different from one species to another; consequently, in 1893 he proposed classifying snakes on the basis of these structures. Many modern herpetologists have used the morphology of the hemipenis as an important tool in snake classification.

COMBAT DANCES

Many species of snakes have been seen in intertwined or elevated head-to-head postures which have been described as courtship dances. In the case of the cottonmouth moccasin (*Agkistrodon piscivorus*) a sort of courtship dance does in fact occur between the male and female in which they intertwine their posterior portions and push and rub their heads together. Most of the other snake dances are combat dances between two males. The males of the Aesculapian snake (*Elaphe longissima*) assume a posture with their posterior halves intertwined and their anterior halves in an elevated loop. In this position they attempt to push each other over with their heads. Male snakes of this species probably were used as the model for the symbol of Aesculapius, the Greek god of medicine. This symbol, the caduceus, is still used as the symbol of the medical doctor.

The most spectacular combat dances are probably those of the large rattlesnakes, including the western diamondback (*Crotalus atrox*) and the red diamond (*C. ruber*). When two males meet, they raise their anterior thirds of their bodies and weave their heads and necks with their tongues flicking. Keeping their heads close together, they entwine their bodies and press or throw their anterior halves at one another until one falls over. They never bite one another, as the fighting is ritualized so as not to be detrimental to the species. The loser departs, but the ramifications of winning are not clear. Some workers have postulated that the snakes are contesting territory, but the admittedly meager amount of work that has been done on snake territoriality suggests that snakes do not maintain and defend a territory. The proximity of a female may provoke snakes to "dance" as mating rivals.

Given the right conditions and stimulation, probably all the larger species of rattlesnakes engage in the male combat dance. It is assumed to be an old and basic pattern of behavior. Genera other than *Crotalus* which have been observed in this activity include *Pituophis*,

Coluber, Elaphe, Lampropeltis, Thamnophis, Drymarchon, Ptyas, Pseudechis, Demansia, Naja, Dendroaspis, Agkistrodon, and *Vipera.* Different species of rattlesnakes have been seen in the combat dance by William Haast, director of the Miami Serpentarium in Florida. Even more interesting was his observation of an eastern diamondback (*Crotalus adamanteus*) and a cottonmouth moccasin (*Agkistrodon piscivorus*) engaged in dancing.

The combat ritual of two male banded rock rattlesnakes (*Crotalus lepidus klauberi*) was recorded on motion-picture film and videotape, and the former was analyzed on a Vanguard Motion Analyzer. The typical actions, postures, and features of the sequence

Combat dance of two male red diamond rattlesnakes (*Crotalus ruber*). This behavior appears to be a ritualistic form of aggression for social communication. The sequence of complex actions, postures, intertwining of their bodies as they rise vertically and sway back and forth has intrigued observers of this elaborate ballet performance. (*Photo: San Diego Zoo*)

of events, many occurring simultaneously, appear to be a ritualistic form of aggression for social communication. The accompanying illustration is descriptive of a typical sequence of the combat ritual as observed by Charles C. Carpenter, James C. Gillingham, and James B. Murphy at the Dallas Zoo. They involve investigation, ascent, vertical display, and final tumbling down to recovery.

SEXUAL DIMORPHISM

A characteristic which consistently distinguishes male from female is said to be sexually dimorphic. Male deer carry antlers; females do not. Female birds are often cryptically colored, while their mates are of brighter plumage. Such traits are rare among snakes but not unknown. An example of sexually dimorphic character in snakes is tail length. The male copulatory organs are housed in the base of the tail. Therefore, male snakes often have a tail which is longer and broader at the base than that of a similar-sized female of the same species. Another difference is in the number and form of the scales on the ventral side of the body, but there is no single general trait for external sex determination.

EGGS

All snakes produce eggs, sometimes as many as a hundred or more. Vipers, boas, and other snakes retain them within their bodies until they hatch. Most snake eggs are oval rather than round, with parchmentlike shells that are less fragile than a hen's egg although more prone to desiccation. For all embryonic snakes, the yolk is virtually the sole source of nourishment. The yolk sac enters the embryo at the umbilicus, where its calcium, phosphorus, and lipoprotein substances are made available to nourish the developing snake. All of the needed calcium for skeletal growth is obtained from the yolk; the shell calcium is not utilized.

The fertilized snake egg has only a single-layer blastoderm (the delicate membrane which lines the impregnated ovum) while still up in the oviduct. This begins its divisions quickly and an embryo surrounded by the amnion membrane soon forms. This membrane is important in that it maintains the developing embryo in a pool of liquid.

Poking from their leathery shells, two infant hognose snakes (*Heterdon platyrhinos*) are about to hatch and be on their own. They will receive no training or protection from their mother. Almost all snakes abandon their eggs as soon as they are laid, or their young as soon as they are born. The babies, about 8 inches long, hacked their way through the shell with an egg tooth hidden beneath their snout. They will feed principally on toads. (*Photo: M. V. Rubio*)

GESTATION

The period of embryonic development varies greatly depending on the species and on temperature. Eggs generally hatch more quickly at higher temperatures. The eggs of the smooth green snake (*Opheodrys vernalis*) hatch within one week, whereas those of many snakes take two or three months. These statistics can be deceiving, however, as they are often more indicative of how long a female retains her eggs in her body than how long the embryos take to develop. There have been unusual cases of a normally egg-laying (oviparous) snake giving birth to live young because of temperature and climate which kept it from depositing eggs. Clifford H. Pope re-

The great role of sexual reproduction in evolution is to promote survival of the species. It shuffles the genes of two parents in the genetic endowment of their progeny and thus exposes a maximum diversity of the characters and capacities of a species to the stringent test of natural selection.

Cape cobras (*Naja nivea*), also known as the yellow cobra in South Africa, usually mate in September and eggs are laid three months later, often underground in a hole or other protected cavity. These snakes grow to an average length of 4½ to 6 feet. (*Photo: SATOUR*)

ported a ball python (*Python regius*) both giving birth to live young and laying eggs.

While egg laying is the most common method of reproduction, some snakes keep the eggs inside the reproductive tract during the embryo stage, and the young are born alive. Reptile eggs that develop inside the mother are quite similar to those that are laid, but lack a calcified shell.

Bearing young alive has several advantages over egg laying. Inside the mother, eggs are protected from predators or environmental dangers such as drying out. Also, the live-bearing snake regulates the body temperature by basking in the sun or avoiding extremes of heat or cold, thus providing a suitable temperature for the developing embryos. Fertilization of eggs normally takes place shortly after mating, but sometimes the sperm may be stored for a longer period, so that several successive broods of young or batches of fertile eggs may result from a single copulation.

The common African python (*Python sebae*) seeks a habitat that is moist, rocky, with nearby wooded valleys, plantations, or bush country, but seldom if ever far from a permanent body of water, for which it has a great love and in which it will lie submerged—with only the nostrils and eyes exposed above the surface—for long periods on end.

FitzSimons records from 30 to 50 (exceptionally up to 100) eggs laid, of which as many as 50 per cent may be infertile. When a female is ready to lay her eggs, she seeks out a suitable secluded spot, such as in tangled brushwood, abandoned ant bear or other animal holes, old termite hills, deep rock crevices, etc. Here the eggs are deposited in a single mass up to a foot in height and covering an area of approximately eighteen inches to two feet in diameter. Around this pile of eggs she immediately curls herself and remains thus, except for almost daily visits to the nearest water, until a few hours before the eggs are due to hatch. (*Photo: SATOUR*)

PARENTAL CARE

The eggs of snakes or the newborn snakes are "left on their own" as soon as the mother lays or gives birth. An interesting exception to this rule is seen in the brooding behavior of some pythons. With these species, the female remains coiled around her clutch of eggs throughout the two-month incubation period. During this time, muscular contractions of the mother's body produce body heat. The contraction rate depends on the temperature of the snake's surroundings; the cooler the environment, the faster the contractions, so that a fairly constant temperature is maintained for the developing embryos.

The king cobra (*Ophiophagus hannah*) may reach a length of 18 feet. These youngsters, which already have an extremely powerful venom and were hatched from a brood of 28 eggs, are now completely on their own. They are shown swimming in a pool at the Bangkok Snake Farm in Thailand, where their venom is extracted and made into serum used to inject snake-bitten patients. (*Photo: Bangkok Snake Farm*)

NESTING

The king cobra (*Ophiophagus hannah*) is unique in being the only snake to construct a complicated two-chambered nest, usually of leaves. One chamber is for the female; the other for the eggs. The male may remain in the vicinity of the nest, and both parents may defend their eggs. Family life among king cobras is not always so harmonious. Herndon G. Dowling recounts a story of Junior, a large male king cobra at the Bronx Zoo, swallowing the first three or four feet of his prospective mate before he and an assistant were able to extract the female from Junior's jaws.

The Chinese mountain viper (*Trimeresurus monticola*) is also known to brood eggs. The mother guards the eggs, but apparently does not build any elaborate nest.

HYBRIDIZATION

The subject of snake hybridization is shrouded in speculation and mythology, although some viable hybrids are known to occur. Perhaps the best-known myth is that western American rattlesnakes (either *Crotalus atrox, viridis,* or *scutulatus*) hybridize with the bullsnake (*Pituophis melanoleucus sayi*) to produce an extremely venomous hybrid that is even more dangerous because it does not bother to rattle. This myth probably arose because of the superficial pattern resemblance between the bullsnake and the rattlers, plus the fact that the bullsnake will vibrate its tail against dried brush or gravel, producing a faint rattle if disturbed. The legend is totally without truth. It would be impossible for these snakes to hybridize, as the bullsnake lays eggs and the rattlers bear live young. Besides, the hemipenes of these snakes are so radically different that the mating would be impossible.

However, a number of rattlesnakes and vipers have produced documented hybrids which are intermediate between the parents in appearance. L. M. Klauber has noted three wild-caught rattlesnakes which were proven to be hybrids. The first was a cross between the eastern diamondback rattlesnake (*Crotalus adamanteus*) and the canebrake rattlesnake (*C. horridus atricaudatus*), the second a cross between the red diamond rattlesnake (*C. ruber ruber*) and a southern Pacific rattlesnake (*C. viridis helleri*), and the third a most unusual intergeneric cross between the pigmy rattler (*Sistrurus catenatus catenatus*) and the canebrake rattler (*C. horridus atricaudatus*). Most of the offspring resulting from zoo hybridizations never attained maturity. In the case of a hybrid between *C. viridis* and *C. ruber* bred at the San Diego Zoo, the male offspring reached maturity but it could not recognize sex, as it courted males and had combat dances with females. The San Diego Zoo also produced offspring from a mating of a Mojave rattlesnake (*C. scutulatus*) and the Aruba rattler (*C. unicolor*).

CHAPTER 4 ~~~~~~~~~~~~~~~~~~~~~~~~~~

Snakes in Captivity

BREEDING SNAKES

In recent years there have been great achievements in the breeding of snakes in captivity, and for many species it has proven to be quite simple. Each year brings new and more regular successes in this field, so that we may begin to look forward to breeding as the norm rather than the exception. However, breeding these animals in captivity was until recently a rare occurrence and there seems to be little widespread knowledge of many of the techniques and parameters involved.

The British Herpetological Society has formed a Captive Breeding Committee to actively encourage captive breeding and promote the keeping of sexual pairs, so that eventually most animals, for either the professional herpetologist or the amateur, will be derived from captive breeding stock. They will also gather together and correlate such information as is derived from the captive breeding of reptiles both in the wild and in the laboratory. This information will be freely available to members on request. Various American herpetological societies are also beginning to place emphasis on snake-breeding husbandry to protect the future of herptiles for systematic scientific studies, educational purposes, or personal enjoyment.

In the United States, Ernie Wagner of the Woodland Park Zoo in Seattle, Washington, and Glenn Slemmer of the University of British Columbia in Canada, have successfully bred, with their combined facilities, the California kingsnake (*Lampropeltis getulus californiae*), gray-banded snake (*L. mexicana alterna*), desert kingsnake (*L. getulus splendida*), Arizona kingsnake (*L. getulus yumensis*), corn snake (*Elaphe guttata*), yellow rat snake (*E. obsoleta quadri-*

vittata), sonoran gopher snake (*Pituophis melanoleucus affinis*), Pacific gopher snake (*P. melanoleucus catenifer*), northern copperhead (*Agkistrodon contortrix mokeson*), Mexican cantil moccasin (*A. bilineatus*), Indian python (*Python molurus molurus*), Burmese python (*P. molurus bivittatus*), and *Boa constrictor*. Some of these species have been bred to the third and fourth generation. During this period of time Dr. Slemmer has produced over 1,000 corn snakes.

The Woodland Park Zoo has a fairly new reptile house, which, as in most zoos, is built for the display of a variety of reptiles to the general public. There are thirty fiberglass cages approximately four feet square with cast-in pools. There are four large walk-in cages for housing pythons, boas, and other large snakes. The reptile collection is typical of what you would expect to find in any good municipal zoo. The heating is forced air, with a background temperature of 75–78 degrees in the daytime, dropping to 72–74 in the evening. Lighting is provided by incandescent lamps and the animals have bred under these for several years. Vita-Lites are used over most of the cages. The wattage is varied depending on the desired temperature for a particular cage. The substrate for most cages is dry sand or pea gravel, and driftwood and plastic plants are used freely in the exhibits.

Ernie Wagner's breeding room at home is in the basement and has a background temperature of 70 degrees in the evening and 75 during the day, except in the winter, when the temperature falls to 60 at night and 65 in the daytime. He uses 25-watt incandescent lights over the cages, and for heat there is a double heat tape attached to the back wall of the aquarium racks. All the cages are pushed up against this tape so that snakes can select their own temperatures, warm at one end of the cage or cool at the other. The heat tapes are attached to a rheostat and turned down as low as they will go. All the cages are aquariums with a substrate of dry fir-wood shavings and every cage has two plastic hideboxes. One of these is on the heated end of the cage and the other is on the cool end, allowing the snakes to hide but not be forced into unwanted temperatures when they do so. The light cycle is varied from 8 hours in the winter to 16 hours in the summer, the same as in the zoo collection. In addition to this area, Wagner has an environmental chamber about two feet square and four feet tall for raising baby snakes in plastic shoeboxes. The temperature in this chamber is a constant 75 degrees and they see 16 hours of light year round. This keeps babies born late in the summer from being exposed to a decreasing light cycle and encourages them to feed through their first winter. Vita-Lites are used in this chamber.

Dr. Slemmer's lab has a background temperature of 72–75 degrees throughout most of the year and no additional heat is provided except for some of the tropical species such as boas, which have a heat tape under their cage. There are cool white fluorescent lights overhead, but the snakes tend to ignore these lights even though they are on late at night in both summer and winter, and prefer the light coming through the windows along one wall as far as reduced winter feeding, gonadal recrudescence, and follicle development in the spring is concerned. The light cycle in this lab is the natural one coming through the window. All of the cages are aquariums or plastic shoeboxes and the bedding is clean newspaper. Plastic hideboxes are provided in all cages.

There are several techniques to induce breeding in temperate and subtemperate snakes. In the wild, environmental factors such as light cycle, temperature, and possibly humidity and an adequate supply of vitamin D_3 may combine to induce reproduction in various species of reptiles. It appears that a changing light cycle and adequate vitamin D_3 supply are the primary inducing factors in most of the temperate species, especially *Lampropeltis* and *Elaphe*. The optimum temperature varies from 70 degrees for most *Thamnophis,* to 75 for most *Elaphe* and *Lampropeltis,* to 80 degrees for most boas and pythons.

The animals are checked for parasites upon arrival and treated and then maintained in the cleanest possible condition, not necessarily sterile conditions but just good, clean, well-ventilated cages with dry bedding, free from excess moisture and old feces. Plaster of paris blocks are maintained in all drinking water as a calcium source. Vitamin D_3 is supplemented orally by putting a small drop of cod-liver oil on each food item fed.

When all of these conditions are met and the animals have had a chance to become adjusted to their individual light cycle and conditions (this may take as long as two years in the case of some snakes, especially if they have been held in other collections), reproductive success may be expected. In the spring of the year as the light cycle lengthens, the ovarian follicles develop in females. Just what time of year this may occur often varies with individual snakes of a given species, depending on what part of that snake's range the individual may come from. This is passed on genetically, so that corn snakes from Florida may cycle in earlier than those from the Carolinas.

As ovarian follicles develop in the female, she becomes increasingly restless until she will eventually be abroad and active during the middle of the day. Any male snakes of the same species, housed in the same room, will also be quite active and restless, attracted by the pheromones being produced by the female at this time. When this behavior is observed, it is possible to pick up the female, hold her gently in a soft cloth in one hand, and palpate the follicles as she crawls through your hand. The follicles will be slightly smaller than marbles, very hard, and will feel like a string of beads passing over the finger which is pressing on her ventral surface. The follicles develop rather rapidly; it is possible to palpate a snake one week and feel nothing and then find fully developed follicles the following week.

From the time of development of her follicles, the female has approximately twenty-one days to locate a male and mate before they will be reabsorbed. Mating should optimally occur within the first two weeks. Matings which occur past 15 or 16 days of follicle development often result in low fertility. After copulation the follicles become larger and nonpalpable as embryogenesis and development occurs.

During the following month additional changes occur in the female, including her going off feed and the absorption of the adipose tissue along the vertebrae, giving her a ridge-backed, pear-shaped appearance if viewed in cross section. Basking under a heat source may frequently occur during this period if one is available. Prior to egg laying a molting will take place, giving a very accurate timing mechanism for calculating the day the eggs will be laid. In 145 clutches of corn snakes in Dr. Slemmer's lab, he observed the range for this pre-egg-laying shed to be 9 to 12 days, with an average of 10 days. Blair's kingsnakes shed 6 to 8 days prior to laying; Arizona mountain kingsnakes, 10 days; Sinaloa milk snakes, 12 days; Great Plains rat snakes 14 days; and Burmese pythons 10 days.

All of these behavioral mechanisms are very useful in determining what is occurring with your own animals and they point out the advantage of a private collection over a public one such as in a zoo. In zoos, the snakes can be given some cover, but need to remain on display. In private collections, with the use of the hidebox many of these mechanisms become quite obvious. If you come into the collection in the middle of the day and all of the snakes are hidden out of sight, everything's normal. If a snake is out and restless, it could mean illness, an impending shed, mite infestation, or possibly a reproductive state, especially if other animals of the same species are active at the same time. At any rate, it is a sure signal that something is going on with that particular animal and it should be investigated.

If good, healthy, parasite-free stock is obtained and kept in cages that are well ventilated, dry and clean, not overcrowded, breeding projects can be successfully undertaken. If there is a musty or moldy smell of old urates and reptile feces, then the cage needs cleaning, no matter how many times it may have been spot-cleaned. Indications that all is not well with your snake include such symptoms as restlessness and respiratory problems, with a mucus buildup and a slight wheezing that is noticeable when the snake is handled. Regurgitation of food and the production of feces that are very liquid, mucoid, and malodorous are other indications that if the situation is not corrected, death will follow, with the snake taking as long as a year to waste away in some cases. Treatment is quite simple, especially if this syndrome is recognized in its early stage. Move the snake to a clean, well-ventilated environment with dry bedding, and put it on a prophylactic tetracycline regimen until the respiratory wheezing clears up.

Wagner cautions against the overuse of vitamins A and D_3, usually administered in cod-liver oil. If your snake appears to be normal, then do not supplement D_3 or do so only at occasional intervals—such as two drops of cod-liver oil once a month for an adult kingsnake or rat snake. A slight dusting of the food with a good, balanced vitamin supplement such as the Squibb product Vionate, which has a balanced ratio of both D_3 and calcium, is appropriate.

The green tree python (*Chondropython viridis*) and the emerald tree boa (*Corallus canina*) are considered to be two of the more remarkable examples of convergent evolution among snakes in the family Boidae. Both are well adapted to a nocturnal arboreal life in tropical rain forests, having strongly prehensile tails, slender compressed bodies, elliptical pupils, and camouflaged coloration. They also possess extremely long teeth for penetrating the feathers of avian prey, which constitutes a good portion of their natural diet along with small mammals and lizards. In addition, they have heat-sensitive facial pits which aid in detecting potential food objects and predators.

Their average adult size is between 4 and 6 feet and the adults of both species share a green coloration which serves to hide them in their forest-canopy habitats.

The juveniles of both species are colored differently from the adults, being a varied shade of yellow or red. The bright coloration of the offspring suggests they may inhabit a different environmental niche from the adults where their bright colors serve to enhance survival amid correspondingly pigmented foliage.

Two most significant differences between *Chondropython* and *Corallus* are their geographical distribution and their reproduction modes. *Chondropython* is an egg-laying python primarily from New Guinea, whereas *Corallus* is half a world apart, being a live-bearing boa from the Amazon region of South America.

BREEDING THE GREEN TREE PYTHON

Breeding snakes in captivity can be a project which requires much time and patience, as well as inventiveness. This is all the more likely when the snake selected for experimental breeding is of a little-known species.

Trooper Walsh, a Washington, D.C., herpetologist and private collector, acquired eight specimens of the New Guinea green tree python (*Chondropython viridis*) for a breeding project. Although this snake, which is also found on Australia's Cape York Peninsula and the smaller islands off Indonesian shores, is not rare in its own habitat, it is encountered only infrequently in zoos and private collections. As a consequence, very little data was available. Walsh set about creating an environment resembling the natural habitat as closely as possible, with special emphasis on temperature and humidity.

Each subject was housed in an individual terrarium, outfitted with bamboo perches, plastic ferns for cover, and water bowls. It was noted that water was drunk from the bowls, and the tree pythons

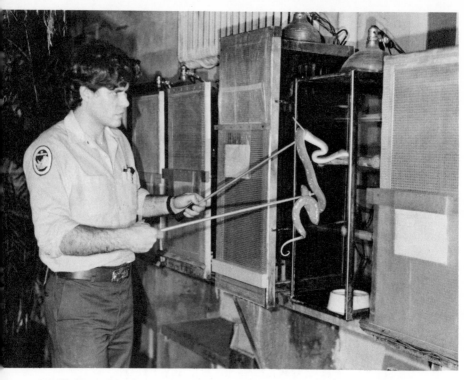

Trooper Walsh carefully manipulates a green tree python (*Chondropython viridis*) into a holding cage at the National Zoological Park. (*Photo: Sheffield Edwards, Jr./NZP*)

also consumed droplets which accumulated on their backs from the moisture provided by daily mistings. The enclosures were heated by 125-watt cables installed in the slate floors. Temperature was regulated by manipulation of polyethylene-covered wooden frames situated on top of the usual wire-mesh lids. When in full covering, or closed position, humidity as well as heat was retained within the terrarium. These lids were moved so that the early-morning temperature of 75 degrees and 55 per cent humidity were gradually increased to 86 degrees and 100 per cent humidity by early evening.

Fluorescent Vita-Lites and white tungsten lights suspended over the top lids (which also allowed penetration of natural light during the day) were switched on via automatic timers, providing a 12-

hour-day cycle beginning at 5 A.M. Red bulbs provided sufficient illumination during the night to manipulate and feed the tree pythons during their active nocturnal hours. Since the presence of internal parasites such as strongyle, tapeworms, and roundworms was noted, Walsh employed appropriate remedies.

Early in August two females and one male were extremely restless during the evening. It was decided to attempt a pairing and the male was transferred to one of the female's enclosure. The female moved all over the cage, followed by the male, who overtook her; the pair intertwined, the male titillated the female's back, then her vent, with his spurs, after which the hemipenis was inserted in the cloaca. Copulation lasted about five hours, then resumed the following night. They separated the following morning.

Since the male of a second pair was inactive, the breeding male was substituted, and over the following two months, the active specimen was moved back and forth from one female to the other. As a consequence, nine breedings occurred between the male and either female. No copulation occurred while either snake was in the process of shedding. However, the male was aggressive following shedding by the female. Most copulation took place during the humid, warm early hours of the evening.

Both females gained weight and by mid-November refused food. A month later, the female first to be bred was transferred to a larger terrarium, which provided more cover and seclusion. Previously active and aggressive, she now preferred to hide and bury her head in her coils. The ends, back, and floor of the cage were made of plywood; the frontal viewing wall was half glass, the remainder was wire mesh covered with transparent plastic, with a canvas flap which could be raised or lowered. The top, which Walsh constructed so that a hinged section could be opened to provide ventilation, was itself hinged and consisted of wooden framework covered with light-admitting polyethylene sheeting. Attached for heating and photoperiod purposes was an incandescent Duro-light, and as in the smaller cage, a red bulb provided illumination during the night hours.

By December 27, the gravid female would prowl the perimeter of her enclosure, and by day would return to her favorite high bamboo perch. Temperature and light cycles were maintained much as in the smaller terraria except that the red light bulb at close range offered some heat at night. Walsh observed and noted (he kept extensive, precise notes throughout the entire project) that her solid-green color had lightened considerably.

Four days later, potential laying sites were constructed and installed. They included two hollow logs, one vertical, the other horizontal, a large plastic bush, and a flat wooden box, 15"×10"×4", which was placed in a corner. These were all investigated by the snake, who would rest in the bush or the box by night but returned to her perch by day.

On January 2 at 10:30 P.M., Walsh observed rippling motions carrying an abdominal mass toward the vent; it was not until ten days later, however, that she entered the hidebox, where she remained. The following night 25 eggs were laid, which were removed and placed in incubators. The snake's color darkened considerably; she accepted food for the first time some ten days later.

All but three of the eggs, tested with a bird egg candler, registered as fertile. They were marked, weighed and measured, and found to average 13.9 grams and approximately 1½" in length by 1⅛" in diameter. Two incubators were constructed from glass terraria. The polyethylene lids were perforated to provide ventilation and the floors were covered with pea gravel to protect plastic egg-holding cups from direct heat emanating from the heating cables below. Water was added and, as it warmed, supplied humidity. Potting soil was placed in the cups in which the eggs, washed with Clorox to prevent mold, rested.

One tank was maintained at a temperature of 83 degrees, the other at 87. In the course of the first few weeks, the eggs in the warmer tank molded and spoiled, indicating that the higher heat and humidity caused them to die.

As for the eggs in the first and somewhat cooler tank, ten began to hatch the first week of March. One, strangled by its umbilical cord, perished, but the others survived as healthy specimens. They were bright yellow with red markings including diamonds, side speckling, red dorsal lines and head markings. The latter were all distinctive and the different patterns made it easy to distinguish one hatchling from the other. All had white tails with black bands. Four were males; five were females. At first they were coaxed into biting and constricting pink mice. Later it was discovered that a mouse held with forceps and pressed against the posterior portion of the body would provoke constriction without biting. The prey then was passed from coil to coil and to the mouth, where it was devoured. Feeding under red light proved most successful.

Walsh was able to conclude that carefully maintained temperature and humidity cycles resulted in conditions highly favorable to breeding, egg laying, and hatching. The artificial climatic conditions approximated those in the natural habitat of the green tree python.

This overall remarkable success was a private project conducted by Walsh. At this writing he is engaged in a similar one with another species, the emerald tree boa (*Corallus canina*), a live-bearing species from the Amazon, being carried out at the National Zoo in Washington, where he works in the reptile department.

BREEDING THE EMERALD TREE BOA

Basically, the environment and cycling techniques employed to breed and maintain *Corallus canina* at the National Zoological Park are the same that were used while working with *Chondropython viridis* in Walsh's home. He "recycled" both species to breed at a time of year when it was most convenient for him to manipulate various environmental cage controls in relation to the seasonal climatic fluctuations and photoperiod of Washington, D.C.

The green tree python breeds during April to June over most of its range in the wild. The emerald tree boa breeds from February to April. Walsh recycled both species to breed from September to December.

The main physical difference between the cage setups for the two species has to do with simplicity. *Chondropython* cages are simple, with little cage furniture or decor, making it easy to maintain. The *Corallus* exhibit at the zoo, on the other hand, is elaborate and more aesthetically pleasing for the public's benefit. The green tree pythons are now kept in individual cages (except during breeding cycles) due to their aggressive dispositions. Specimens have been known to attack, mangle, and kill cage mates. The boas are generally more sociable and are housed together at the zoo throughout the year without any problems.

The fact that *Chondropython* is an egg layer (known gestation periods of 75–120 days) which broods its eggs (incubation period of 48–52 days), while *Corallus* is a live-bearer (known gestation periods in excess of 250 days), means that one must "pamper" the boa at least twice as long as a gravid tree python. Many problems or complications can develop in a gravid snake, particularly with species as delicate in captivity as these two, according to Walsh.

Chondropython apparently has very specialized thermal requirements for developing viable eggs.

At the National Zoological Park, particular care is given to the gravid female's preferences at different stages of gestation. Extreme temperatures are avoided by means of a brooding chamber containing a thermal gradient; the gravid female chooses her thermal basking sites according to her needs. All of the green tree python's eggs hatched without mishap.

LIFE EXPECTANCY

The ages of wild-caught snakes cannot be reasonably estimated beyond their third or fourth year of life. Generally, a snake that is large for its species is old, but how old cannot be determined. Herpetologists do not know enough about natural death rates from predation, disease, and old age to predict how long a species will live in the wild. Consequently, our estimates of life spans for various species must be extrapolated from age data on captive snakes. It is not known for sure whether any wild snakes would exceed our maximum known ages for captives. In the case of very large snakes such as anacondas and pythons, which have virtually no natural enemies, it is possible that they might survive longer in the wild than our zoo records indicate.

LONGEVITY

The oldest individual snake on record is a 41-year-old *Boa constrictor constrictor* at the Philadelphia Zoo which was an adult when captured. It is therefore reasonable to assume that some boids may reach age 50 or more. A female anaconda (*Eunectes murinus*) lived for more than 31 years at the Basle Zoo, Switzerland. The greatest recorded age for a viperid snake is 30+ years for a timber rattlesnake (*Crotalus horridus*), also a wild-caught adult, with a northern copperhead (*Agkistrodon contortrix mokeson*) having lived for slightly less than 30 years at the Philadelphia

Reputedly the largest of snakes, the anaconda (*Eunectes murinus*) of South America has lived for over 30 years in captivity. (*Photo: Roy Pinney*)

The timber rattlesnake (*Crotalus horridus horridus*) still survives in the northeastern United States despite the destruction of large areas where it was once numerous. They vary in coloration from a velvet black phase to light yellow, brown, or gray. They have been kept in captivity for over 30 years. (*Photo: Roy Pinney*)

Parental care is nonexistent once the eggs are hatched or the young are born alive. Although young snakes may congregate in numbers near their birthplace, they are strictly on their own.

This cluster of week-old boa constrictors may contain an individual that may reach 10 feet in length or live to a reported maximum life span of 41 years. (*Photo: M. V. Rubio*)

Zoo. Colubrid snakes generally do not live as long, although some of the larger rat snakes, kingsnakes, and bullsnakes survive over 20 years in captivity and an indigo snake lasted 25 years. Life spans of elapids in captivity are very variable from one species to the next. American coral snakes lived for about 7 years and an African black-lipped cobra (*Naja melanoleuca*) for 29 years after hatching at the San Diego Zoo. It should be noted that some species of snakes do not adjust as captives and therefore their longevity records may not be indicative of their situations in the wild.

SEXING SNAKES

Determining the sex of a snake is sometimes difficult even for experienced herpetologists. Generally, female snakes have shorter tails than males of the same species. Male snakes usually have a broader tail base than females.

Efforts to breed snakes in captivity require accurate sexing of the mating pair. This may be done by gently inserting a long, thin, blunt, lubricated rod into the cloaca toward the tip of the tail. In females the probe will not penetrate for more than 3 subcaudals into the tail. In males, however, the probe will slip easily into a pocket on each side of the tail and penetrate from 8 to 16 subcaudals in most snakes. Extreme caution must be taken when inserting the probe, as too much force can injure the snakes, especially females.

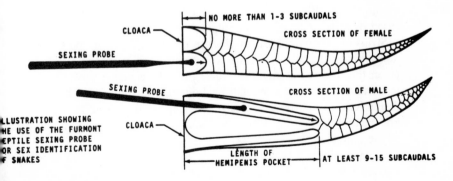

(Illustration: Furmont Reptile Equipment)

Poisonous snakes should be placed in a plastic tube for safe handling.

Jozsef Laszlo has determined some guidelines for selecting the proper size of probe. For best results it is important that the probe not be too large or too small. Either extreme could be harmful to the animal. A 5-foot ball python (*Python regius*) would use a 4-mm. probe, a 6½-foot Texas bullsnake (*Pituophis melanoleucus sayi*) would use a 3-mm. probe, a 3-foot California milk snake (*Lampropeltis triangulum*) would use a 2-mm. probe. Snakes under 2½ feet would use a 1-mm. probe. Boas and pythons 7–9 feet or larger use the 5½-mm. probe. The most often used probes are the 2- and 3-mm. sizes manufactured by Furmont Reptile Equipment, Seabrook, Texas.

FOOD

Captive snakes can be difficult to feed and some may refuse to eat altogether. Few snakes insist upon live food. In fact, many snakes that refuse to feed on live animals readily take to eating dead ones. Live animals are time-consuming to keep, create odors, and are not always available.

Animals left in a snake cage overnight may burrow into inaccessible places or may even attack and kill the snake, particularly if they are hungry and food pellets are not provided. Food items may include mice, rats, hamsters, guinea pigs, rabbits, chipmunks, squirrels, and even bats. Chicks, sparrows, pigeons, and other birds that may have been injured during migration or D.O.R.'s found along a highway may readily be consumed. Surprisingly, some snakes will eat highly putrified food which may have been left in a cage and refused by other, more particular eaters.

Strips of raw beef, parts of chicken or fish will readily be taken by many kinds of snakes, particularly if this food is in some way first given the scent of a snake's natural prey. One might leave the food in a mouse or rat cage for half an hour or rub the food over the rodent's hair. A diet built exclusively of this kind of food is, however, not recommended since it lacks many of the nutrients found in whole animals.

In cases where a snake continually refuses to eat any kind of food, environmental factors should not be overlooked. For most snakes, a temperature of 75 to 85 degrees is good; 90 degrees is excessive and less than 70 degrees is too low. Snakes may also refuse to eat if they are subject to cage vibration, noise, light, and constant movement of people or objects outside the cage. After a snake has eaten it should always have available a dark, quiet place in which to digest its food.

Other factors to be considered are humidity, which should be kept below 60 per cent, a changing daily cycle of light and darkness, hideboxes, cages of adequate size and not too crowded. There are no generalizations that can be made about any one species concerning habits; different individuals may have different traits. Most snakes refuse food during the opaque state preceding shedding; gravid females may fast during gestation; species that normally hibernate during the winter months, particularly if obtained from the wild before cold weather, often refuse to eat and may be inclined to starve themselves.

Food items may be quickly killed by ether, drowning, or freezing, and placed in the home freezer, conveniently packaged in a long polyethylene tube or plastic bag, closed tightly with rubber bands or a bag sealer. Before feeding, all food items should be thoroughly thawed for several hours. Food still frozen and swallowed by snakes may cause gastrointestinal disorders such as diarrhea, arrested digestion, fermentation of the stomach contents, and other ailments.

HAND-FEEDING

Snakes are capable of starving themselves to death. In some cases the cause of this behavior can be pinned down and remedied—an illness may be cured or environmental factors may be changed. But if all else fails, "hand-feeding" may be the answer.

One simple way to hand-feed harmless snakes involves no more elaborate equipment than one's finger and a file card. Fold the card in half, dip the folded corner in warm water, and slip it through the hole in the snake's rostral plate. Then slide the folded edge toward the hinge of the snake's jaw and push the food down the card and into its throat.

For feisty or dangerous snakes another method works better, as recommended by Charles W. Radcliffe. Place the snake to be fed into a plastic or glass tube (making sure that the ends of the tube

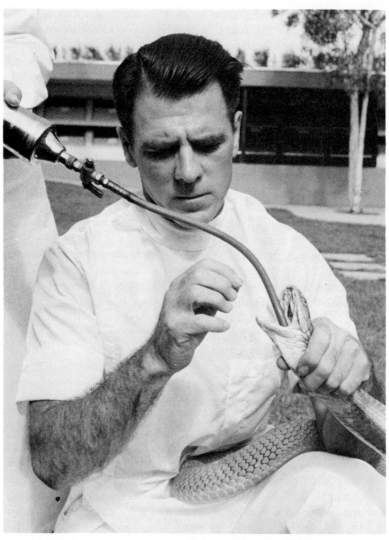

With a "secret formula" of his own concoction, Bill Haast at the Serpentarium in Miami, Florida, has kept his captive snake collection in prime condition by using only forced-feeding methods. An appropriately sized catheter-type flexible tube is gently inserted down the reptile's gullet. A caulking-type gun or veterinary syringe carefully controls the dosage of vitamin-added nourishment. (*Photo: Roy Pinney*)

are smooth) which is 33–50 per cent the length of the snake. The internal diameter of the tube should be about 1.5 times the diameter of the snake, or slightly wider than the width of the snake's head if it is greater than the body diameter. Once the snake's head has reached the opposite end of the tube, grasp the snake firmly to prevent it from crawling through and pushing its head completely out of the tube.

The food item should have a diameter .5–.65 times that of the snake and should be gently shoved into the snake's mouth and to the back of the throat. If the tube diameter has been well chosen and the snake has not been allowed to push its head through the tube opening, then it should be able to swallow the food item while in the tube but be unable to disgorge it. The snake should remain in the tube until swallowing is well underway.

The advantages of this method are: (1) a tight grip on the snake's neck is not necessary once it is in the tube; (2) the tube holds the body straight to facilitate swallowing; (3) nothing is forced down the snake's digestive tract for any distance; and (4) risk to the handler is minimized if a venomous species is being fed.

BREEDING INSECTS

In the case of small insect-eating snakes, the disadvantages of using living food are minimal, for insects are abundant and easy to raise. One all too common insect used for feeding purposes is the cockroach. There are four species found around the house or available from suppliers if you can't seem to find any. Each species should be raised separately. The *German* and *Brown-backed* cockroaches are small and brown, averaging about one half inch in length. The Germans have two dark streaks on their thorax. The Brown-backeds have two brownish-yellow stripes crossing the base of their wings. Black *Oriental* and reddish-brown *American* cockroaches are larger —about one to one and a half inches in length—and easily distinguished from each other.

Wide-mouthed gallon jars, fitted with 50-mesh bronze or nylon screen covers, are used for rearing and maintenance. As a further precaution against escape, apply a smear of petroleum jelly along the inner rim of the jar. Roll up a yard-long, six-inch-wide strip of corrugated cardboard loosely inside the jar for the roaches to hide in and place food in a two-inch-diameter feeding cup or cylinder made of the same material. A water source is most important and can be made as follows: Obtain a vial four inches high and two inches in diameter and make a hole in the cover about three quarters of an inch in diameter. Then fashion a cotton "wick" by winding string or thread around most of its length and forcing the loose end up through the hole. The cotton should be made somewhat wider than the hole to ensure a snug fit. Fill the vial with water and put inside the big jar.

Roaches will eat almost anything, but dry dog chow, which has rough surfaces, is ideal and will not decay. Keep the jar at a temperature of from 75 to 85 degrees. Water from the wick will keep up the humidity, and a single food and water supply will last several weeks.

For those who have a special aversion to roaches, a very good alternative is the cricket. Crickets have a soft exoskeleton and may be easily trapped in the backyard in summer or bought from a local pet shop year-round. However, they do kick up something of a racket at night and require more space to culture than roaches.

To trap crickets, place a wire-screen cone over a wide-mouthed jar, small end (about one half inch in diameter) down. Fruit or peanut butter placed in the jar as bait should be changed daily. Set a few of these traps under bushes or in tall weeds and collect the crickets when you change the bait.

A five-gallon aquarium with a wire-screen lid is an adequate container for rearing. Divide the container in half with a few rocks and add to one side a slightly damp mixture of dirt, peat, and peat gravel in equal parts. A thin, flat board placed over part of the mixture will allow crickets to crawl about underneath and will help to retain moisture. Layer the other half of the tank with dry sand and place two shallow dishes on it for food and water. Ground rat chow or chicken mash makes good food. A few pebbles should be placed in the water dish since crickets invariably fall in and may drown.

Always leave several males and females in the tank for continued reproduction. The females are distinguished by the dark spearlike ovipositor protruding backward from the abdomen.

Within a few weeks, very small, young crickets will be produced by the hundred. These will mature in 30 days at 90 degrees or considerably longer at room temperature. You will find it necessary to transfer the young crickets to a larger enclosure for maturing. This can be a screen-topped 30-gallon aquarium or a garbage can. Be sure to add food, water, and a supply of egg cartons or rolled-up cardboard to this container for them to hide under.

NUTRITION

The role of nutrition in the successful maintenance of reptiles has been of particular concern to Fredric L. Frye. Some generalities can be made with respect to the preferred foods of a few snake species.

(1) Boas, pythons, rat snakes, gopher snakes or bullsnakes, and vipers all prefer warm-blooded prey such as rodents and/or birds of the proper size.

(2) Garter snakes, water snakes, etc., will usually take fish, frogs, toads, earthworms, slugs, etc. Dead food frequently will be accepted. Often these species can be induced to accept mice if fish or worm slime is applied to the fur.

(3) Indigo snakes, kingsnakes, etc., will eat both warm-blooded prey and poikilotherms (organisms whose temperature depends on their environment).

(4) The smaller ringneck or brown snakes and their kin will usually confine their diet to small salamanders, earthworms, and small snakes or lizards.

(5) The racers, vine snakes, etc., will usually accept lizards. These need not be alive and can be provided from a frozen supply in the off season when ready availability cannot be assured.

(6) Some snakes, such as the king cobra, are almost strictly snake eaters. Again, frozen snakes may be utilized after they have been thawed.

WATER REQUIREMENTS

Although many reptiles, especially desert and pelagic or coastal marine species, possess active salt glands to aid in water conservation, all should be supplied with a source of fresh water which is compatible with their living habits. Many reptiles will only drink by lapping up water on leaves as they would following a rain.

FOOD PREFERENCES OF SNAKE SPECIES

* = usual food

o = occasional food

SNAKE	SMALL MAMMALS	BIRDS	OTHER SNAKES	LIZARDS	EGGS	FROGS, TOADS SALAMANDERS TADPOLES	FISH	INSECTS	WORMS	SLUGS
Anaconda	*	*					*			
Boa, Python	*	*								
Boomslang	*	*	*	*						
Coachwhip	*	*	*	*						
Cobra (except King Cobra)	*		*	*						
Coral			*	*		o				
Copperhead	*	*		o						
DeKay's										
Egg-eating					*				*	*
Garter	*		*	*		*	*	*	*	*
Gopher, Bull, Pine	*	*		o	o					
Green				*				*		
Hog-nosed						*				
Indigo	*	*	*	*		*				
Kingsnake	*	*	*	*						
King Cobra	o		*							

SNAKE	SMALL MAMMALS	BIRDS	OTHER SNAKES	LIZARDS	EGGS	FROGS, TOADS SALAMANDERS TADPOLES	FISH	INSECTS	WORMS	SLUGS
Krait	*		*	*		o				
Mamba	*	*								
Mangrove	*	*		o						
Marine or Sea							*			
Night			*	*						
Racer	*	*	*	*	o	o				
Rainbow						tadpoles				
Rat or Chicken	*	*			*					
Rattlesnake	*	*		o						
Ribbon						*	*			
Ring-necked						salamanders				
Vine Snake				*					*	
Viper, misc.	*	*	o	o						
Water moccasin	*	*	*	*		*	*			
Water snake, misc.	o		o	o		*	*		*	o

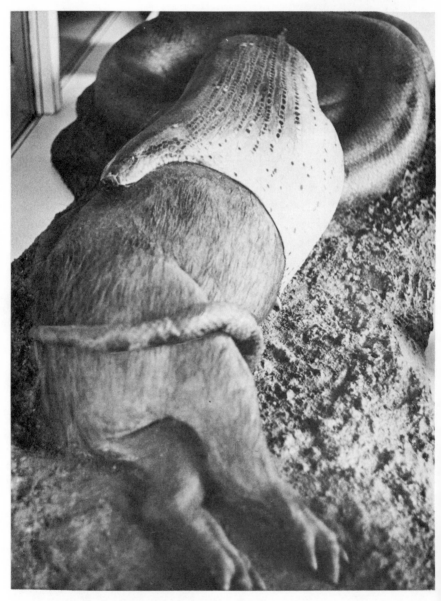

An anaconda (*Eunectes murinus*), the largest of the giant constricting snakes, is shown swallowing a pig. (*Photo: Senckenberg Museum*)

INANITION

Inanition, the physical condition which results from complete lack of food, afflicts captive snakes. As stores of body fat and muscle are catabolized, the eyes sink, the skin shrivels, and the bones become prominent. In such a state of virtual starvation and dehydration, resistance to stress is almost nil. Gentle handling and a quiet environment of a suitable temperature are almost as essential as nutritional replacement.

The quickest, most efficient method for immediate restoration of positive lipid (fats), protein, and vitamin balance is by tube-feeding with a nutritional-replacement product that has a high-calorie, low-bulk formula designed for convalescent animals, such as Pet Kalorie or Nutrical. These products may be mixed with pureed infant-food meat diets. A urethral catheter of appropriate size, or an infant-feeding tube, works well for intubation. Both will fit on a syringe with a Luer tip to be fastened.

If the patient is not eating voluntarily for a month or two, Dr. Frye suggests that attempts to hand-feed a natural diet (young mice, rats, baby chicks, etc.) should be made. Food for snakes may be lubricated with beaten egg. The mouth is opened and small amounts of food are introduced and advanced down the esophagus with a smooth-tipped flexible probe. Plastic artificial-insemination pipettes are ideal for this purpose. Gentleness is essential! The snake's body should be well supported during handling.

OBESITY

Although the majority of nutritional difficulties in captive animals are directly associated with malnutrition, insufficiency of total digestible nutrients, or vitamin-mineral deficiencies and/or imbalances, a percentage of these animals will be found to be suffering the effects of too much caloric intake for their particular metabolic requirements. It is not uncommon for a zealous amateur herpetologist to overfeed his pets in an effort to see how fast they can be induced to grow. Without sufficient energy demand on the reptile's metabolism, excess food is stored as fat deposits. If this situation continues for enough time, fatty infiltration will become noticeable.

Whereas most snakes should be fed once weekly, a meal every three weeks might be more suitable for large pythons and boas. Fasting may be quite prolonged in some reptiles without causing serious effects if the water consumption is adequate to allow for normal renal function. Reptiles have been reported to fast for as long as 36 months without appearing to suffer deleterious effects but such lengthy periods of fasting represent the extreme.

The snake that ate a snake that ate a snake!

There was an Egyptian cobra (*Naja haja*), which swallowed an Egyptian cobra, which swallowed a house snake (*Boaedon lineatum*), which swallowed a bird.

The snake that started the cycle was a harmless house snake which had swallowed a bird. The house snake was then swallowed by a 3-foot Egyptian cobra which in turn was swallowed by a 5-foot Egyptian cobra. W. D. Haacke of the Transvaal Museum inspects the specimens. (*Photo: SATOUR*)

CANNIBALISM

Some degree of cannibalism in snakes is essentially normal. Many snakes are ophiophagous—that is, they eat snakes, including their own species!

Overcrowded conditions, with the resultant stress of high population density, probably are the major inciting cause of cannibalism. Reducing the population and providing hiding places will usually eliminate this problem. Prey species obviously must not be housed with their predators.

ADDITIONAL DISORDERS

Calcium-phosphorus imbalance may be remedied by injections of calcium gluconate two or three times weekly, oral vitamin D_3 and calcium supplementation, change of diet, sunlight radiation or artificial ultraviolet lamps such as Grolux or Vita-Lite. Hypovitaminosis C responds to ascorbic acid dosages of 25 mg. or more.

FLOOR COVERING

There are varied individual preferences regarding the proper floor covering for snake cages. Whatever is chosen, it should be some absorbent material which can be easily changed when soiled. Layers of newspaper or wrapping paper, cardboard, wood shavings, wood chips, aquarium gravel (No. 3 grade), or an outdoor carpeting material that is washable, such as Astroturf, all have been used successfully.

Ordinary clay or marl soils, most grades of sand, including that used for building or industrial use or from the beach, are not recommended. Cedar chips or shavings have been found to be toxic to some reptiles. Dead leaves, sphagnum moss, and Spanish moss may harbor mites or other parasites. Large stones or pebbles and pine bark are not satisfactory because they allow excretions to accumulate.

A long-handled, wide-cupped cooking spoon or a garden or plasterer's trowel is useful in removing areas containing fecal matter.

Cages for snakes may be as elaborate or "natural" as the keeper desires, but the basic requirements for most species can easily be met. Essential are a water dish, a hidebox, a floor covering which can easily be kept clean, and some sort of temperature control. Cages may be the inexpensive aquariums with tight-fitting covers, wooden or plastic containers with adequate ventilation, or this built-in enclosure. Snakes can escape from astonishingly small openings. (*Photo: Roy Pinney*)

DISEASES OF SNAKES

H. G. Dowling stresses a practical approach to reptile diseases. If we consider any factor that adversely influences the health of animals as disease, many things, other than a parasite or disease-causing organisms, come into focus. "Because, let's face it, the treatment of reptilian diseases is still pretty much in the stage of witch doctor practice."

Keeping snakes in an enclosure which is not well ventilated may produce problems regarding the health of the animal. One may decide to keep water snakes in relatively damp enclosures but doing so will produce sores on the belly, blisters on the skin, and they may soon die. Apparently, all except a very few highly developed water snakes must get out and sun themselves, and get perfectly dry in order to counteract the bacterial and fungus infestations that thrive under damp conditions.

Dr. Dowling stressed that the temperature of the environment can exert the most dramatic effects on the health of reptiles. Most of us, as warm-blooded animals, might feel cool, or might feel hot, but it doesn't affect us significantly unless the change is of very high intensity. But entire life processes of reptiles are based on the temperature of their surroundings. If it is too cold, snakes will rarely eat. If they do, they are not able to digest their food. A dramatic example of this happened at the Bronx Zoo when attendants moved some of their cobras from their normal quarters to quarters that were outside a temperature-controlled space, so that the thermometer never got below 70 but didn't get up to 80 degrees either. For the first couple of weeks the cobras seemed to be doing fine. They all ate, and then, three weeks later, they all regurgitated undigested mice. They were on the fine line of their temperature requirements—able to carry on what appeared to be normal processes, eating in the low 70's, but unable to digest that same food at those temperatures. When the temperature was raised to 80, then they not only ate but they also digested.

Sunlight provides not only heat but ultraviolet rays that at least in humans help to transform chemicals into vitamin structures and aid health in other ways. We are not sure that this happens in reptiles; herpetologists do not seem to agree about it. Many snakes that do not do well in captivity may require a change in temperature that corresponds to that of their environment in the wild. Temperatures may get down to about 50 degrees at night and rise to perhaps 80 degrees during the day. Perhaps this explains why snakes which hibernate during the winter months are difficult to keep at household temperatures, which are so much warmer than outdoors.

Despite the best of care, snakes, like other living things, often become diseased. This is manifested by listlessness, weight loss, lack of appetite, and dehydration as indicated by loose tenting of the skin. When this is noticeable, sanitation should be improved—fecal matter should be removed without delay, and water dishes boiled or disinfected with Clorox or alcohol. Phenol, cresol, and other coal-tar derivatives are highly toxic and should be avoided.

Reptiles can be treated with some of the common antibiotics. There seems to be better response to antibiotic therapy if the ambient temperature is kept elevated at 85–90 degrees.

During the physical examination, a snake should be held firmly, but not too tightly, immediately behind the head, and its body should be supported. If held dangling by the neck too long, it can suffer damage to the spinal cord or circulatory difficulty because of inability to return systemic venous blood to the heart while in the vertical position.

QUARANTINE

To ensure the longevity of snakes in captivity, a newly acquired specimen should temporarily be kept in quarantine, not immediately introduced to a cage containing other snakes. If the specimen is not too large, a wide-mouthed gallon jar is suitable. Holes should be punched upward through the cover so that the snake does not rub its rostral plate while seeking to escape. Larger specimens may be contained in larger aquaria or in garbage cans which have tight covers to prevent escape. Water sufficient to cover the coiled snake will drown some of the ectoparasites or force them to congregate around the head, which the snake will keep above water. Ticks, mites, etc., may be easily seen and removed.

TICKS AND MITES

A commercially available organic phosphate known as No-Pest Strip insecticide, manufactured by Shell Chemical Company, has proven effective in eliminating the snake mite (*Opionyssus serpentina*) from its host and cage enclosure.

Originally designed to kill flies and mosquitoes and other small insects for up to four months in an enclosed area, the product comes in a foil package and sells for about $2.00 at hardware stores and supermarkets.

Chemically, the active ingredient is 2.2-dichlorovinyl dimethyl phosphate with inert ingredients equivalent to 20.0% w. technical Vapona insecticide.

The damage a tick does is not very great. It may irritate the area and it takes some blood from the snake, but no reports have been noted where disease transmission has been linked to these reptilian parasites.

DYSECDYSIS

Difficult, painful, or fragmented moulting of the skin may be ameliorated by soaking the snake in an inch or two of tepid water for fifteen minutes. The snake should be placed in a cloth bag first. Examine the skin and eyes of snakes for incomplete shedding. Normally, the eye caps, or spectacles, are shed with the rest of the outer layer of epidermis. Incompletely shed skins or eye caps should be gently removed because the underlying tissue is injured by overzealous peeling and readily becomes infected.

RESPIRATORY INFECTIONS

Pneumonias may be caused by viruses, bacteria, fungi, yeasts, protozoa, and chemical irritants as well as by conditions which place an unusual stress upon the animal. Symptoms appear during the course of the disease. The snake may be sneezing or wheezing, with its mouth and throat full of clear, slightly viscous saliva which foams from the lips. The snake is still strong but usually refuses to feed. In later stages the snake is noticeably weaker with mouth-open breathing, feces may be blood-streaked, sticky, foul, and sparse, gums may be mottled. The terminal stage is approaching when a snake appears to be losing coordination, acts very weak and flaccid, with head held high, and gapes for long periods at a time, its mouth full of purulent yellow phlegm though its nostrils remain generally clear. There is weight and strength loss during this severe stage which contributes to the snake's final demise. However, the snake is still curable during this period. Q-Tips dipped in Betadine will help wipe away the mucous infection. Gentamycin Sulphate (Schering), high doses of vitamin C daily, and injection of fluids have been found effective.

TAPEWORMS

Tapeworms are ordinarily not a problem unless they occur in huge numbers. They live very comfortably within the host and don't really cause a great deal of difficulty. There are one or two exceptions. Instead of merely clinging to the inside of the intestine as most tapeworms do, some may burrow their heads into the wall of the intestine. This obviously causes some problems.

Scolaban, Anaplex, Wormcap, or Ripercol tablets have been found helpful in the treatment for tapeworms.

MOUTHROT

A common and troublesome disease in captive snakes is ulcerative stomatitis, commonly called mouthrot or cankermouth. Injuries to the mouth, particularly when caused by snakes' striking against the glass or wire of their cage, predispose to this disease. Two organisms that have been incriminated as causing the infection are *Aeromonas hydrophilia* and *Bacillus fluorescens liquefaciens,* which produce deep inflammation of the jawbone and oral cavity.

The first sign of ulcerative stomatitis in snakes is the appearance of a frothy bubbling around the lips and in the mouth. The animals then refuse to attack live prey or eat. Within a week, flecks of white or yellowish-white caseous masses are seen in the mouth area, the snake becomes steadily weaker, and death follows. Spontaneous recovery is infrequent.

Diseased snakes should be isolated from unaffected ones. Several prophylactic treatments with effective antibiotics or chemotherapeutic agents should be given to all cage mates of affected snakes. Contaminated cages should be cleaned and sterilized before re-use. Quaternary ammonium disinfectants are suitable for this purpose.

Dr. Leonard C. Marcus of the Albert Einstein College of Medicine, Bronx, New York, recommends an application of 25 per cent sulfamethazine, hydrogen peroxide, or other mild antiseptics. The dead tissue should not be removed too vigorously because fresh tissue may be exposed to further invasion. Because snakes in this condition refuse to eat, they should be carefully force-fed through a tube attached to a hypodermic syringe. A mixture of finely ground liver mixed with raw egg, some milk, and a pinch of vitamin and mineral supplement in modest amounts has been successfully used by the author.

CHAPTER 5 〜〜〜〜〜〜〜〜〜〜〜〜

Venomous Snakes

There are fewer than 2,500 species of snakes known today. Of these, slightly over 400 are venomous, only half of which are dangerous to man. If we were to further narrow the list to snakes which actually are responsible for human deaths with any regularity, we would be left with only a few species that cause most of the fatalities. Leading such a list would be Russell's viper (*Vipera russelii*), the attractive-looking but most feared snake of India, Burma, and Thailand; the cobras and kraits of southeastern Asia; the puff adder (*Bitis arietans*), found throughout Africa; the vipers of the genus *Bothrops,* abundant in South America; and the rattlesnakes, found primarily in the United States.

More people die from automobile accidents each year in the United States than from snakebites throughout the world. More die from the bite of a bee, wasp, or hornet than from a venomous snake. Even poisonous spiders contribute twice as many fatalities as snakes. The odds are literally greater of being killed by lightning!

It is widely held that a venomous snakebite is, unless treated, almost always lethal. The popular imagination pictures many dire and lurid consequences of snakebites, including such grotesqueries as immediate convulsions, quick paralysis, blindness, and death within an hour. Fewer than one person in every fifteen bitten by a *venomous* snake dies as a result. This is partially due to the availability of snake antivenin and other methods of treating bites. One more statistic, even more startling, should place the danger in proper perspective. Among healthy American adults and teen-agers who are bitten by venomous snakes and are *not* treated, only one in eight dies as a result, and only a small percentage of the survivors show any lasting ill effects.

This is not to imply that a rattlesnake is not dangerous or that it

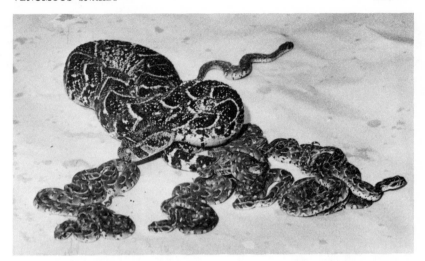

A puff adder (*Bitis arietans*) photographed soon after giving birth to 28 young snakes in the Durban Snake Park, South Africa.

These snakes are ovoviviparous and the young are born in a thin, membranous sac from which they escape by giving sharp twists and turns. Within ten minutes they are alert, puffing vigorously when disturbed, with a very toxic bite potential. (*Photo: James Hutton/ SATOUR*)

can be as safely played with as a cocker spaniel pup. The danger is real enough and only experts should have anything to do with them. A large percentage of fatalities in the United States are a result of playing a Russian-roulette type of gambling game by handling a venomous snake as a pet. Rashness in this matter is twice as bad as excess temerity.

The potential beneficial uses of snake venom keep a number of scientists occupied with experiments. Obtaining venom is an important job and techniques have been developed to perfect it. Milking a snake is as simple as it is dangerous. All one has to do is grab a viper behind its head, so that it cannot strike, manipulate the head properly to bring down the fangs, then gently press the areas around the venom glands to squeeze the valuable and lethal liquid out.

Several laboratories and institutions around the country keep ven-

At Snake Park, Port Elizabeth, South Africa, a lecture demonstration with venomous cobras and puff adders. (*Photo: SATOUR*)

omous snakes for just this purpose. The men who milk the snakes are fully trained experts, yet often enough they are bitten. The most important use of snake serum remains, ironically enough, the making of antivenin. The process is rather simple and is based upon the same principles that produce serums for treating rabies and preventing polio. The human body has the ability to fight most alien elements introduced. It does this by producing antibodies. A weakened dose of polio virus injected into a person causes that person's body to produce an antibody that overcomes the polio virus. Afterward, if an individual is attacked by polio, the antibodies are already in the bloodstream and ready to go to work.

Antivenin is simply the antibody produced in a horse's bloodstream after the animal has been injected with increasingly larger doses of snake venom. When injected into the victim of snake poisoning, the antibodies go to work immediately to neutralize the effects of the venom. Some serums are specific for a certain species of snake. Others are a combination of several antivenins; these are called polyvalents and are used when the species inflicting the bite is unknown.

VENOM

Venomous snakes have apparently existed since the Miocene Epoch, more than 20 million years ago. The elapids and viperids are both believed to have arisen from the more primitive colubrids, some of which have developed venom as well. The evolution of venom conferred great selective fitness upon the viperids and elapids, as it allowed them to kill large struggling prey with minimal risk to themselves. It also gave them a formidable defense weapon. The vast majority of venomous snakes use their venom to subdue their prey and many use it for defense as well.

Venom itself is usually yellow in color, being lighter in most elapids. Among the components found in most or all venoms are: hyaluronidase, which destroys the matrix of connective tissues; ribonuclease, which destroys RNA, the cell's protein-making genetic material; deoxyribonuclease, which destroys DNA, the genetic material of all animal cells; phosphodiesterase, which breaks the molecular bonds of many important cell components; and ATPase, which

A homemade improvised L-shaped snake hook is being used to pin down the head of an eastern moccasin (*Agkistrodon piscivorus piscivorus*) before picking it up. (*Photo: M. V. Rubio*)

destroys the cell's major energy-carrying molecule, ATP (adenosine triphosphate). The hemotoxic venoms of the viperids are high in proteinases which cause hemorrhage and necrosis of living tissue. All of the elapid snakes tested have been found to have cholinesterase in their venoms, a substance which interferes with neural transmission.

The symptoms of snakebite differ markedly depending on the nature of a species' venom. Among the symptoms often seen in viperid bites are swelling, pain, sloughing of skin and tissue, weak or erratic pulse, extravasation of blood from the vessels, hemorrhage, shock, nausea and vomiting, thirst, weakness, and necrosis of tissue. Elapid bites are usually less painful, and are characterized by drowsiness, drooping of the eyelids, a feeling of thickening of the tongue, difficulty in swallowing and breathing, headaches, blurred vision, paralysis, pain in the abdominal region, nausea, and vomiting. The venom of the most dangerous rear-fang, the boomslang (*Dispholidus typus*), is hemotoxic and causes massive internal bleeding.

Certain species of snakes, including the Mojave rattler (*Crotalus scutulatus*), are known for their tendency to deliver "dry" bites in which little or no venom is injected. Such behavior should not be taken lightly, however, as these snakes are capable of delivering a full venom load if the "dry" bite does not succeed in deterring an attacker.

For detailed accounts of venom and its actions, the reader is urged to read Klauber and Minton and Minton.

The question of the "deadliest" or "most dangerous" snake is often raised by laymen and professionals alike and certainly makes interesting cocktail party conversation. Many snakes are capable of inflicting a lethal bite and survival may depend on an individual's sensitivity to a particular venom, the size of the snake, the amount of venom injected, and the immediate availability of first aid and antivenin. There are a number of snakes whose bites are most feared, and these are worthy of mention.

YIELD AND LETHALITY OF VENOMS OF IMPORTANT
POISONOUS SNAKES

Snake	Average length of adult (inches)	Approximate yield, dry venom (mg.)	Intraperitoneal LD_{50} (mg./kg.)	Intravenous LD_{50} (mg./kg.)
North America				
A. Rattlesnakes (*Crotalus*)				
Eastern diamondback (*C. adamanteus*)	33–65	370–720	1.89	1.68
Western diamondback (*C. atrox*)	30–65	175–325	3.71	4.20
Timber (*C. horridus horridus*)	32–54	95–150	2.91	2.63
Prairie (*C. viridis viridis*)	32–46	25–100	2.25	1.61
Great Basin (*C. v. lutosus*)	32–46	75–150	2.20	—
Southern Pacific (*C. v. helleri*)	30–48	75–160	1.60	1.29
Red diamond (*C. ruber ruber*)	30–52	125–400	6.69	3.70
Mojave (*C. scutulatus*)	22–40	50–90	0.23	0.21
Sidewinder (*C. cerastes*)	18–30	18–40	4.00	—
B. Moccasins (*Agkistrodon*)				
Cottonmouth (*A. piscivorus*)	30–50	90–148	5.11	4.00
Copperhead (*A. contortrix*)	24–36	40–72	10.50	10.92
Cantil (*A. bilineatus*)	30–42	50–95	—	2.40
C. Coral snakes (*Micrurus*)				
Eastern coral snake (*M. fulvius*)	16–28	2–6	0.97	—
Central and South America				
A. Rattlesnakes (*Crotalus*)				
Cascabel (*C. durissus terrificus*)	20–48	20–40	0.30	—

Snake	Average length of adult (inches)	Approximate yield, dry venom (mg.)	Intraperitoneal LD_{50} (mg./kg.)	Intravenous LD_{50} (mg./kg.)
B. American lance-headed vipers (*Bothrops*)				
Barba amarilla (*B. atrox*)	46–80	70–160	3.80	4.27
C. Bushmaster (*Lachesis mutus*)	70–110	280–450	5.93	—

Asia
A. Cobras (*Naja*)				
Asian cobra (*N. naja*)	45–65	170–325	0.40	0.40
B. Kraits (*Bungarus*)				
Indian krait (*B. caeruleus*)	36–48	8–20	—	0.09
C. Vipers (*Vipera*)				
Russell's viper (*V. russelii*)	40–50	130–250	—	0.08
D. Pit vipers (*Agkistrodon*)				
Malayan pit viper (*A. rhodostoma*)	25–35	40–60	—	6.20

Africa
A. Vipers				
Puff adder (*Bitis arietans*)	30–48	130–200	3.68	—
Saw-scaled viper (*Echis carinatus*)	16–22	20–35	—	2.30
B. Mambas (*Dendroaspis*)				
Eastern green mamba (*D. angusticeps*)	50–72	60–95	—	0.45

Australia
A. Tiger snake (*Notechis scutatus*)	30–56	30–70	0.04	—

Europe
A. Vipers				
European viper (*Vipera berus*)	18–24	6–18	0.80	0.55

Indo-Pacific
A. Sea snakes				
Beaked sea snake (*Enhydrina schistosa*)	30–48	7–20	—	0.01

An eastern diamondback rattlesnake (*Crotalus adamanteus*) yielding some of its venom as demonstrated by Ross Allen. (*Photo: Ross Allen Associates*)

The snake with the largest venom yield is the eastern diamondback rattlesnake (*Crotalus adamanteus*) of the southeastern United States. The dried venom contained within its venom glands may exceed 700 milligrams. The venom is only of moderate potency, however. The intravenous LD_{50} (in mg./kg.) for mice (the amount which

The eastern diamondback rattlesnake has been recorded to a length of 8 feet, making this an "ominously impressive snake to meet in the field; suddenly finding yourself in close proximity to the compact coils, broad head, and loud buzzing rattle is almost certain to raise the hair on the nape of your neck," according to Roger Conant. They are found throughout Florida, north to North Carolina, and west to Louisiana. Rabbits, rodents, and birds are their chief diet. (*Photo: Max Schiffer*)

kills 50 per cent of the test mice) is 1.68. The cascabel (*C. durissus*) is generally believed to be the most deadly rattlesnake. It yields only 20–40 mg. of venom, but 10 mg. may be sufficient to kill an adult. Because horses cannot produce adequate antibodies for its venom, at least 10 ampoules of antivenin are needed to treat its bite. Over 50 per cent of those bitten die without treatment. Such rattlesnakes usually do not inject all of their venom, but often inject up to 50 per cent.

The tic polonga, Russell's viper (*Vipera russelii*), is often credited with causing more bites than any other single species. It kills many people in India, Ceylon, and Burma. It yields up to 250 mg. of venom, and it is estimated that 40–70 mg. will cause death.

The black mamba (*Dendroaspis polylepis*), despite its name, is seldom actually black but a dark brown. In South Africa it is the largest and most feared of the venomous snakes because of its uncertain temper. Average length of adults is 10 feet. Usually 12 to 14 eggs are laid at a time. A newly hatched young may measure from 15 to 24 inches and, within an hour or so of birth, be quite capable of killing mice, rats, etc. Under favorable conditions, mainly a plentiful food supply, growth is extremely rapid, with a length of 6 feet recorded in a year. (*Photo: SATOUR*)

The black mamba (*Dendroaspis polylepis*) of Africa is not a major cause of snakebite, but it is the second-largest of all venomous snakes, the fastest known snake, and able to strike almost half of its body length. It produces copious amounts of extremely potent neurotoxic venom, enough to kill a half dozen men. Its bite is almost always fatal if antivenin is not administered.

The Indian krait (*Bungarus caeruleus*) is one of the most feared snakes in India. The lethal venom dose for a human is only a few

VENOMS PRICE LIST

The following prices are quoted in U.S. Dollars per gram

CROTALIDAE

Ancistrodon bilineatus	.50.
Ancistrodon c. contortrix	.40.
Ancistrodon c. laticinctus	.50.
Ancistrodon p. piscivorous	.20.
Ancistrodon p. leucostoma	.30.
Ancistrodon rhodostoma	.75.
Bothrops atrox	.40.
Bothrops nasuta	.70.
Bothrops n. nummifer	.80.
Crotalus adamanteus	.40.
Crotalus atrox	.30.
Crotalus c. cerastes	.100.
Crotalus d. durissus	.50.
Crotalus d. terrificus	.50.
Crotalus h. horridus	.30.
Crotalus h. atricaudatus	.35.
Crotalus ruber	.60.
Crotalus scutellatus	.95.
Crotalus v. viridis	.50.
Crotalus v. helleri	.50.
Lachesis muta	.300.
Sistrurus catenatus tergeminus	.70.
Sistrurus miliarius barbouri	.40.
Trimeresurus popeorum	.100.
Trimeresurus wagleri	.200.

ELAPIDAE

Bungarus caeruleus	.160.
Bungarus candidus	.250.
Bungarus fasciatus	.80.
Bungarus multicinctus	.175.
Dendroaspis angusticeps	.80.
Dendroaspis jamesoni kaimosai	.150.
Dendroaspis p. polylepis	.150.
Dendroaspis v. viridis	.150.
Hemachatus hemachates	.50.
Micrurus fulvius	.500.
Naja flava [Naja nivea]	.50.
Naja h. haje	.30.
Naja h. annulifera	.50.
Naja hannah [Ophiophagus hannah]	.70.
Naja melanoleuca	.30.
Naja n. atra	.50.
Naja n. siamensis	.30.
Naja n. siamensis [light phase]	.30.
Naja n. sputatrix	.50.
Naja nigricollis	.30.
Naja nigricollis mocambique	.30.
Naja nigricollis pallida	.50.
Naja nivea [Naja flava]	.50.
Notechis scutatus niger	.500.
Ophiophagus hannah [Naja hannah]	.70.

HELODERMATIDAE

Heloderma horridum	.200.
Heloderma suspectum	.300.

BOIGINAE

Dispholidus typus	.800.

VIPERIDAE

Atheris squamigera	.400.
Bitis arietans	.40.
Bitis caudalis	.300.
Bitis nasicornis	.60.
Causus rhombeatus	.60.
Echis carinatus sochureki	.100.
Vipera r. russellii	.50.
Vipera r. siamensis	.40.

A SAMPLE AND COST ANALYSIS OF VENOMS OF SPECIES NOT LISTED CAN USUALLY BE PRODUCED WITHIN THIRTY TO NINETY DAYS.

A current price list of venoms from Biotoxins, Inc., produced at their facilities in St. Cloud, Florida 32769. (*Chart: Biotoxins, Inc.*)

milligrams and a majority of bites are fatal even with antivenin treatment. It is known for its curious habit of biting almost exclusively at night.

The small 18-inch saw-scaled viper (*Echis carinatus*) has a venom which is highly toxic to man. It is found in both North Africa and Asia and is an important cause of snakebite death. Apparently only a few milligrams of its 30-mg. venom reserve can cause death, which may occur as long as two weeks after the bite. It produces massive hemorrhaging. Antivenin is available.

The Gaboon viper (*Bitis gabonica*) is the largest viper, being very

The taipan (*Oxyuranus scutellatus*) is a coppery or dark brown snake with a yellow belly that appears to be most abundant around rocks, where it lives in rodent burrows. When provoked it flattens its head, compresses the neck vertically, and expands the body so that the white skin shows between the scales. It arches its body, waves its tail, and then attacks so swiftly and suddenly the victim may be bitten several times before he can defend himself or escape.

Few people survived its bite before a specific antivenin (Taipan) was produced by the Commonwealth Serum Laboratories of Australia. (*Photo: Australia News Bureau*)

heavy and up to 7 feet long. Its two-inch fangs can inflict a bite which is usually lethal without treatment. Fortunately, it is seldom encountered and is very difficult to awaken during the day.

Australia is unique in being the only continent where the majority of snake species are venomous. It possesses three species which are among the most deadly in the world. The death adder (*Acanthophis antarcticus*) is a small elapid which may produce nearly 100 mg. of venom. Over half its bites are fatal if they are not treated. The tiger snake (*Notechis scutatus*) produces less venom, but only a few milligrams can produce a fatal bite. The taipan (*Oxyuranus scu-*

The Australian tiger snake (*Notechis scutatus.*) is the most dangerous snake of southern Australia. Adults are 4 to 5 feet long, with a record 8 feet recorded. Ground color varies from yellowish, greenish gray, orange, and brown to black. It is active at night and not aggressive until molested. The greatest danger appears to be from stepping on the snake in the dark. Often there are few local effects from the bite, but as noted in *Poisonous Snakes of the World,* a manual for use by the U. S. Amphibious Forces, Department of the Navy, Bureau of Medicine and Surgery, the systemic effects are swift and grave.

A specific antivenin (Tiger Snake) is produced by the Commonwealth Serum Laboratories of Australia. (*Photo: Australian News Bureau*) *tellatus*) is a very large Australian elapid, reaching a length of 10 feet. It is considered to be one of the most potentially dangerous snakes in the world, as bad as or worse than the black mamba, although it does not account for many bites. Until the development of an antivenin, virtually all taipan bites were fatal.

Finally, the most deadly sea snake is the 3–4-foot beaked sea

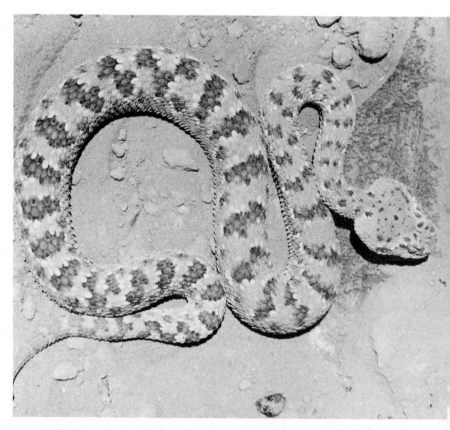

Milligram for milligram, the venom of the saw-scaled viper (*Echis carinatus*) is said to be the most toxic. Found in the desert regions of North Africa, western Asia, India, and Ceylon, the snake is usually less than 2 feet in length. It rubs the sides of its coils against one another to produce a sharp rasping sound. This specimen was photographed in Israel. (*Photo: Roy Pinney*)

snake (*Enhydrina schistosa*). It is believed to possess the most toxic venom of any snake, only 1.5 mg. being required to kill an adult human. As it possesses up to 15mg. of venom in its reserve, it is quite dangerous. It is responsible for more fatal bites than all of the other sea snakes combined, although it usually does not bite unless provoked.

Although many snakes on the Indian subcontinent kill more people than does the king cobra (*Ophiophagus hannah*), it is a very dangerous animal nonetheless. Its venom is exceeded in potency by many other elapid snakes, but is produced in copious quantity. There are few documented cases of king cobra envenomation, as the

The king cobra (*Ophiophagus hannah*) is found in southeastern Asia and the Philippines, attaining a length of 16 to 18 feet. The great size is an important recognition feature; the large occipital shields is another. It is not common. If cornered or injured it can be very dangerous. When angry it gives a deep resonant hiss similar to the growl of a small dog. (*Photo: Chris Hansen*)

king eats other snakes rather than rodents, so it is not found in populated areas. In two documented cases of king cobra envenomation, neither person survived half an hour. The king cobra's venom yield of up to 500 mg. is the highest for any elapid snake.

Not as large as the Gaboon viper, its close relative, the puff adder (*Bitis arietans*) kills more people than any other African snake. Its venom yield approaches 200 mg. and a large puff adder carries enough venom to kill half a dozen men. It is a snake of widespread distribution and is quite common within its range. Although puff adder bites are often lethal, death does not occur for a while after the bite, sometimes as much as twenty-four hours, and there is often more time available for antivenin to be secured than in the case of a Gaboon viper bite. Puff adder bites cause massive internal and external hemorrhage.

INCIDENCE OF VENOMOUS SNAKEBITES

Accurate information on the incidence of venomous snakebites is difficult to obtain because many doctors do not report milder bites, many people report nonvenomous bites as venomous, and in many parts of the world, including more remote areas of the United States, no records are kept at all. Statistics can be misleading anyhow, as the locality in the United States which has reported the most bites is the Miami Serpentarium, where the director, Bill Haast, has been bitten over a hundred times.

A study done for the World Health Organization estimated that there were 30,000 to 40,000 deaths annually from snakebites. Since most bites are not fatal, we can deduce that there are hundreds of thousands of envenomations each year. Taking into consideration the fact that snakebite is not investigated at all in some of the more primitive countries where it is most common, it is possible that there are a million bites each year.

Dr. Henry Parrish has done an admirable job of compiling statistics for the United States. He concludes that approximately 6,700 snakebites are treated annually in the United States. Envenomation is highest in children and teen-agers, unlike the situation in most other parts of the world, where adults account for most bites. Fortunately, only about a dozen people die. Texas and North Carolina have the highest incidence of venomous snakebite. It should be

The long-nosed viper (*Vipera ammodytes*), readily identified by the up-turned snout, has an average length of 25 to 30 inches. It inhabits the dry hilly country at an elevation between 2,000 and 5,500 feet in south-eastern Europe and Asia Minor.

It is largely nocturnal but sometimes climbs onto bushes to bask in the sun. Generally thought to be the most dangerous of the European vipers. (*Photo: M. V. Rubio*)

noted that a substantial percentage (perhaps 25 per cent) of the re-ported bites involve professional or amateur herpetologists or reptile dealers, and some of the deaths are accounted for by bizarre religious snake-handling cults whose members refuse treatment if bitten. The vast majority of bites in the United States are caused by rattlesnakes. An occasional death is attributed to the cottonmouth and coral snake. Copperheads, which account for many bites, are rarely capable of killing an adult human.

Southeast Asia has always had the greatest number of snakebite

Demonstration showing effectiveness of "snakeproof" leather boots. Fangs are unlikely to penetrate legs so protected. (*Photo: Ross Allen*)

fatalities of any region. The mortality figure for India alone is usually figured in excess of 20,000 annually. Thousands more die yearly in Burma and Bangladesh.

Central America is another area traditionally high in snakebite fatality. Several hundred people die of snakebite annually in Mexico alone. The barba amarilla (*Bothrops atrox*) is the major cause of fatalities in southern Mexico and Central America.

It is thought that 1,000 people or more die annually from

The red-lipped snake (*Crotaphopeltis hotamboeia*) of South Africa, 2 to 3 feet long, is probably one of the best-known and most widespread snakes in Africa, because it is frequently found in gardens. Owing to the comparatively low potency of the venom and the fact that the fangs are set so far back in the mouth, the bite of this snake is more or less harmless to man. To ensure the full effect of the venom on its prey, this snake does not let go after biting but holds on and chews the flesh of its victim, according to V. M. FitzSimons. (*Photo: John Pitts/SATOUR*)

snakebite in Brazil, with the cascabel (*Crotalus durissus*) and species of *Bothrops* being the major offenders.

Despite the high incidence of very dangerous snakes in Africa and Australia, snakebite mortality is low. This may reflect the low population densities of much of these continents, or a general awareness of venomous snakes on the part of the people. There are apparently fewer than 1,000 deaths annually in all of Africa, and the number of fatalities in Australia per year seldom exceeds eight. Europe has few dangerous snakes and has about the same fatality rate as the United States.

It should be noted that there are extensive areas in the world where there are no venomous snakes, including much of northern Canada and the U.S.S.R., Maine, Alaska, Chile, all of the Greater Antilles, most of the smaller Caribbean islands (except Martinique, St. Lucia, Trinidad, Tobago, and Aruba), Madagascar (rear-fangs are present), New Zealand, and the entire Atlantic Ocean and the Mediterranean Sea.

COBRAS AND CHARMERS

The front-fanged snakes grouped under the name "cobra" are the most feared—and also the most revered—in the world. The name itself conjures up an Indian bazaar, colorful, crowded, and noisy.

The haunting melodies of the charmer's pipe sift upward into the thick air as from the basket before him the strangely beautiful hooded head appears. The crowd collects about this mysterious man and his charmed serpent, and watches with rapt attention as the reptile weaves and hisses. The cobra seems hypnotized by the charmer. Its head moves ominously, yet it does not strike, and a ripple of astonishment moves through the crowd. The music stops, and the snake drops back into the basket. Coins shower about the charmer's feet, he expresses his gratitude, takes up his basket, and moves off to another part of the teeming bazaar, another crowd, another performance.

It is an impressive show, even when the observer knows it is compounded more of mumbo jumbo and chicanery than of courage and skill. It is a performance that has stirred more speculation and controversy among herpetologists than any other ancient snake ritual. Are the snakes rendered harmless before the performance begins?

A cobra spreads its hood as it emerges from a basket when the top is
suddenly removed. Actually, the snake is not aggressive and for "snake
charmers" performing their act the possibility of a bite is not likely.
(*Photo: Jack Muntzner/Staten Island Zoo*)

Does the charmer indeed know some profound secret that gives him mastery over this deadly creature? Or is it mere chance that charmers survive? Might they not be fatally struck at any instant?

These questions cannot be answered with certainty. But even to discuss them with any assurance we must know more about the famed and fabled cobra—and we must dispel many of the myths that surround it.

The elapids are widespread. Members may be found on every continent with the possible exception of Europe. In the United States the family is represented by the colorful coral snakes. In Africa there are several cobra species, including the black "spitting" cobra, and the famous Serpent of the Nile which Cleopatra clasped to her breast in suicide. A majority of the venomous Australian snakes are members of the cobra family, including the death adder.

India and other parts of southern Asia have several cobras in addition to the common spectacled cobra, which is the focal point of most cobra lore. The king cobra, the largest venomous snake in the world—the species may grow up to 18 feet long—is not even found in India proper. Rather it makes its home in the Philippine Islands and the coastal regions of Southeast Asia. The several snakes found in India that are called kraits are also common, and, some naturalists believe, account for more deaths than the common cobra.

Cobras are not vipers; that is, they do not have movable fangs. They belong to the group of elapids, venomous snakes with immobile fangs that are much shorter than the fangs of the vipers. We know that the most effective strikers among the poisonous snakes are the vipers. By comparison, the cobras are rather clumsy. They can strike only downward, and must keep their fangs embedded in the victim for several seconds in order to eject a sufficient quantity of venom. The venom itself is usually of the neurotoxic variety, and in most cases it is more deadly, drop for drop, than the hemotoxic venom of the vipers.

The most immediately noticeable feature of the cobras is the hood. The name cobra itself derives from the term *cobra de capella* ("hooded snake"), used by early Portuguese explorers to describe the snake they found in Asia. While the exact purpose of the hood is unknown, it is generally displayed when the snake is excited or aroused. Some herpetologists believe that, like the rattles of the rattlesnakes, the hood is the cobra's way of saying, "Don't tread on

COBRA FACTS AND FIGURES

COMMON NAME	SCIENTIFIC NAME	GENERAL RANGE	APPROXIMATE SIZE OF ADULT	MAXIMUM KNOWN SIZE
King Cobra; Hamadryad	*Ophiophagus hannah*	Peninsular India to the Philippines and the East Indies.	9 to 10 ft.	19 ft. 3 in.
Indian Cobra	*Naja naja*	India to southern China, the Philippines, and the East Indies.	4 to 5 ft.	6 ft. 7½ in.
Oxus River Cobra	*Naja oxiana*	Turkestan, from the Oxus River Valley to the Caspian Sea.	Probably 5 ft.	?
Morgan's Cobra	*Naja morgani*	Persia, Iraq, and Syria.	Probably 5 ft.	?
Egyptian Cobra	*Naja haje*	Northern rim of Africa, and from both sides of the Red Sea south through East Africa to Angola and the Transvaal.	5 ft.	8 ft. 6 in.
Black Cobra	*Naja melanoleuca*	Tropical Africa south of the Sahara.	6 ft.	8 ft. 7½ in.
Yellow Cobra	*Naja nivea*	South Africa.	5 ft.	6 ft. plus
Black-necked Spitting Cobra	*Naja nigricollis*	Tropical Africa south of the Sahara; not known from the lower Congo River Basin.	4 to 5 ft.	7 ft. 8 in.
Ringhals (Spitting Cobra)	*Hemachatus haemachatus*	South Africa.	3 ft.	4 ft. 5 in.
Water Cobra	*Boulengerina annulata*	West and Central Africa.	5 ft.	8 ft. 7½ in.
Innes's Cobra	*Walterinnesia aegyptia*	Egypt.	4 ft.	?
Gold's Tree Cobra	*Pseudohaje goldii*	Central Africa.	5 ft.	7 ft. 10 in.
Guenther's Tree Cobra	*Pseudohaje nigra*	West Africa.	5 ft.	7 ft.

(Table: Carl F. Kauffeld)

me!" Others have suggested the hood is part of the bluffing mechanism of many snakes, a warning to would-be attackers that the snakes may be dangerous. This theory is supported by the fact that several harmless snakes have hoods, which they use, it would seem, to capitalize upon the fear of cobras evident in many animals—including human beings.

There are several good reasons for the high incidence of cobra bite fatalities. First, there is the propensity of cobras for visiting men's dwellings. The diet of the cobras consists largely of small rodents, lizards, and other snakes that are found most often where men have put up buildings. Occasionally, travelers to India report finding the serpents even in modern buildings, but such occurrences are rare. The cobra has little trouble gaining access to the ill-constructed homes of most native Indians, however. Further, in most places in India supplies of antivenin are not immediately available, and the neurotoxic venom of the cobra is extremely fast-working.

Still another reason for the large number of deaths in India is, indirectly, the heat of the Indian day. This causes many Indians to do their traveling at night, and a good deal of this traveling is on foot over ill-marked, narrow footpaths. In addition, the majority of Indians are often without shoes, and the loose covering they wear offers no protection for the lower legs. Walking ill-clad in the dark over narrow paths is an invitation to a "defensive" cobra strike.

In most parts of the world where dangerous snakes live, men carry on a never ending battle with them, and usually with some degree of success. This accounts for the ever lower number of snake-poisoning deaths in the United States. (Unfortunately, it also accounts for the extermination of many harmless and useful snakes, a fact that must be regretted by all admirers of nature.) In India, however, the cobra is considered a holy animal, and most Indians believe that killing cobras is sinful. Thus, snake-control programs are not possible, and the majority of Indians will not kill a cobra even after being bitten.

There are two different reasons for the reverence with which Indians treat cobras. The first is the Hindu belief in reincarnation. Hindus believe that the spirit of a person after death is reborn in some animal, often a cow or a cobra. Killing either of these creatures amounts to slaughtering one's own ancestors and so it is not done.

The second reason is based on an elaborate myth that accounts also for the "spectacles" which mark the hood of the Indian cobra. Hindus believe that the powerful god Krishna once visited the earth in the guise of a mortal. After some time the god became tired and lay down to sleep. When he awoke he found a cobra which had spread its hood to protect the god from the burning-hot sun. The god blessed the cobra and touched it upon the hood with two fingers. The "spectacles" are the result of that divine touch, and to this day the cobra is held to be sanctified by Krishna. When the god is portrayed, a cobra is always shown forming a protecting umbrella over him.

Once a charmer has a snake he is in business, and the word "business" is used advisedly. The Hindu snake charmer is a showman pure and simple. He is the P. T. Barnum of the Orient, part con man, part performer. His show is just that—a show put on by a skilled showman for pay in the form of tossed coins.

That is not to say that the snake charmer is a fraud. The dangers are real, and before hitting the tourist circuit, the charmer must have had years of practice.

Indian snake charmers belong to a closed society. They are just one of the many different castes, or classes, that make up the Indian people. The snake charmers live in villages scattered throughout India, but also frequent the suburbs of the big cities and tourist centers. The son of a snake charmer does not think of being anything but a snake charmer, just as the son of, say, a carpenter or farmer never dreams of becoming a snake charmer. The children born in the snake charmers' villages begin their training early, accustoming themselves to the snakes belonging to their fathers, uncles, and neighbors. (Snake charming, traditionally, is a male occupation.)

After capturing his cobra, the snake charmer sets out. He finds himself a street corner in Bombay, New Delhi, or Calcutta, sets himself down on his haunches, and begins playing his exotic, haunting melody. Soon a crowd of tourists and locals has gathered and the show can begin. The lid of the basket is removed, and out comes the snake, hood spread and hissing. The crowd shrinks back in fear, but the charmer seems to have things under control. The music fills the air, and the snake dances and weaves. Then the show is over. The snake drops back into the basket. The lid is replaced. The coins fall.

The show is only partly a fake. It is a fake in that the snake is not charmed. When the charmer removes the lid of his basket, he usually gives the basket several taps which the snake can "hear." It rises instinctively, and the charmer adjusts the rhythm of his melody to that of the snake, not vice versa. The snake continues swaying because it is attracted by the movement of the charmer's shoulders. The reason it does not strike is that the charmer stays just out of range.

The "charmed" cobra is really acting in a perfectly natural manner. The snakes used are not even semi-tamed. In fact, charmers must take a vow to release caught snakes within a certain period— usually one to six months—and charmers insist that new-caught snakes are the best showpieces; veteran cobras, it seems, become indolent and refuse to respond to the charmer's basket-tapping. The penalty for breaking the vow, the charmers believe, is to be bitten by the snake.

Snake charming as a career has more than its share of occupational hazards, for at least part of the show is "for real"—the snakes used usually are healthy and capable of inflicting mortal strikes. Some observers have contended that the cobras used by the charmers have been in some way incapacitated. The charmers, they say, sew the snakes' mouths shut, or remove the fangs or poison glands. While this may happen in some cases, usually it does not, and for good reasons.

Remember that cobras are revered in India. Anyone harming a cobra commits what amounts to a serious crime in the eyes of most Indians. Taking away a cobra's ability to poison amounts to sentencing the snake to slow death by starvation. The Indians would not permit this to happen, a fact the charmers, who are already under attack by the more "modernized" elements of Indian society, are well aware of. Moreover, it would be extremely difficult to render a cobra harmless and remain undetected. Removing the poison glands would leave the snake clearly maimed. Sewing the mouth shut is equally detectable. Removing the fangs would accomplish little, for they would quickly grow back. All fanged snakes shed their fangs regularly, and behind each fang grows a number of new fangs which can inflict damage. Even if the budding fangs were removed with the full-grown ones, it would not necessarily prevent a fatal bite. The poison would still flow, and all the cobra would have to do would be to break the victim's skin with its remaining teeth.

Thus, the charmer's show is not really a fake. There is a real and ever present danger that the show might be the last the charmer will put on. Indeed, the mortality rate due to snake poisoning is rather high among snake charmers. They always carry with them a shiny black stone, said to be spewed by a frog buried alive, that, when applied to a snakebite wound, is supposed to absorb venom. That, however, as many snake charmers have discovered too late, is merely wishful superstition.

Why aren't even more snake charmers killed by their dangerous little showpieces? For one thing, in order to inject enough venom to kill a man, the cobra's strike must be both true and long-lasting. A charmer, unless he gets careless, can usually avoid this type of bite.

Also, the cobras chosen by the charmer are well selected. Not every cobra will do. Many, when disturbed, will rear up, strike once, then crawl away. These are unsuitable for the charmer's purpose and are released. Only those that will remain attentive during the entire performance are retained.

Indians are not the only snake charmers in the world. In fact, variations of the Hindu art occur in almost every underdeveloped area of the world where snakes are common. In Burma the snake charmers use only the larger, much more deadly king cobra, and heap scorn upon their Indian comrades who use the lesser spectacled cobra. They add insult to injury by performing such feats as kissing their "charmed" pets. How they survive that one can be ascribed only to the fact that they lead a charmed life.

In Africa, where the cobra family is represented by several species —including the mamba, one of the most lethal snakes in the world —snake charmers also find ready audiences. In addition to their shows they hire themselves out as snake removers, guaranteeing that after they have gone through a house no snakes will remain.

It is the African black cobra which does most of the "spitting" ascribed to its family. Many explorers and naturalists have recorded the effects of having the snake's venom enter their eyes. Almost always, if the venom is washed out promptly, the damage is only temporary.

RATTLESNAKES

Very few Americans would think of boasting that we have more rattlesnakes than any other place in the world, yet it is a fact that the United States and Mexico have virtually a monopoly of the rattlesnake population. Only two species are found in Central and South America—one of them confined to the little island of Aruba off Venezuela—the rest of the 30 species and 65 subspecies are shared about fifty-fifty with our good neighbor below the border, and because they are unknown in the Old World they can be said to be 100 per cent American—as American as Bourbon and corn pone. Every state in the Union except Maine, Alaska, Hawaii, and Delaware has at least one species; some, like Arizona, as many as eleven species.

Fascinating to scientist and layman alike, these snakes with rattles on their tails show more diversity than most people would think possible. Some grow to giant size like the eastern and western diamondbacks, both of which are known to exceed 7 feet and are suspected of reaching 8 feet. If we were to go to certain mountain ranges in the Southwest we would find species that seldom exceed 18 or 20 inches, such as the Arizona twin-spotted rattlesnake. It and its neighbor the ridgenose or Willard's rattlesnake rarely leave the forested mountaintops; seldom found lower than 6,300 feet, they are usually encountered around 7,000–8,000 feet. Rattlers exhibit vast differences in colors and markings, and their distinct habitat preferences distribute them over every type of terrain we have in our country. There are those which restrict themselves to southern pine flatwoods and swamps, others that occur only in mountains, in the East and the West; still others are found only in tableland and deserts of the West and Southwest—the prairie rattler, sidewinder, tiger and speckled rattlesnakes.

The southern pigmy rattlesnake (*Sistrurus miliarius*), one of the smallest of North American pit vipers, and consequently among the least formidable to man, nevertheless possesses a potent poison and fangs long enough to pierce a man's skin, and so should be treated with caution.

The rattle of this snake is so small that its effective sound range is only a few feet. Its rattling has occasionally been confused with insect noise. Found in dry sandy areas, as are many other rattlesnakes, this species, when aroused, thrusts its head in the direction of the disturbance in a most pugnacious manner. Yet, it should be reiterated, it would rather elude a man than fight him.

Though most rattlesnakes feed exclusively on warm-blooded animals, the southern pigmy will take frogs in addition to small rodents and birds. It produces up to thirty-two young viviparously.

I have found that the massasauga (*S. catenatus*) tames rather readily in captivity. It seldom shows its displeasure by rattling, and feeds well on small birds, mice, and frogs, preferring different foods in different seasons, like the copperhead. It gives birth to relatively tiny living young in small numbers. It is found most often in swampy areas and seems to have generally (except for its rattles) more in common with moccasins and copperheads than with rattlesnakes.

About an hour's drive from New York City, I can still find timber rattlesnakes (*Crotalus horridus*) sunning themselves in or near their dens during the months of May and September. They will sometimes remain still to avoid detection or glide away as they make their warning rattles. They gather in limited numbers in late summer and early fall in preparation for hibernation. When springtime comes, they emerge from the deep fissures, and remain clustered in this area during the mating season. In the hot days of summer they disband and are to be found in the nearby timbered regions. Despite their migratory habits, they are not particularly nomadic, and in any given season will not wander far away from their favorite haunts.

The same snake in the swamplands of the southern states is rather different in its habits. Known as the canebrake rattlesnake (*C. horridus atricaudatus*), it is more docile and grows considerably larger.

The timber rattlesnake, like most rattlesnakes, is partial to warm-blooded food, particularly rabbits, birds, mice, rats, and squirrels. It produces up to a dozen living young, and in one litter may be found examples of both the black and yellow phases of the species no matter what color the mother happens to be. The baby snake, which emerges around the middle of September, is approximately a foot long. If well fed it grows rapidly. Like other snakes, it is independent from birth, being equipped with its complete and functional venom apparatus from the moment it enters the world.

The eastern diamondback rattlesnake (*C. adamanteus*) is the largest venomous snake in North America. Because of its size, temperament, and the potency of its venom, it is among the most dangerous. Growing to lengths in excess of 7 feet, boldly patterned with diamonds on its back, few snakes are as awesome and impressive. This is the snake that is most often the center of horror stories. Yet, as always, the truth falls far short of the myth. Certainly the eastern diamondback rattlesnake is responsible for the deaths of human beings; but such occurrences are still rare enough so that when it happens the story is front-page news. And, as is so often true with venomous snakes, the danger is not to hikers in the woods, but rather to the careless collectors who fail to exhibit sufficient respect for their dangerous trophies.

Yet it must be noted that this species is far less withdrawing than most snakes. Unless shelter be quite close at hand, the snake, upon being disturbed, will assume a defensive position. The body coils in a concentric circle. The body inflates with air and the tail vibrates restlessly, causing the rattles to give forth their eerie sound which mingles with the snake's hissing. This snake will not strike at random, but rather carefully waits for an opportunity to sink its fangs. If come upon in its wanderings it will attempt to disappear in the underbrush and I have scrambled after them on many occasions unsuccessfully. If escape is thwarted it assumes the defensive position at once without hesitation. Its courage is second to that of no other snake.

Early in April, several dozen herpetologists who have been impatiently awaiting spring collecting, make an annual pilgrimage to a snake stamping ground in a game preserve in South Carolina. Some hitchhike, others arrive by bus, car, or motorcycle or fly down in their own planes. Armed with a snake hook or clamp-tongs and a few heavy cotton bags ranging from large pillowcase size down, one is equipped to bag his prey. The hook may be an angle iron attached by one side to a wooden handle about four feet long or a grass cutting scythe with the sharp blade removed leaving a spring-steel right angle or, best of all, Pillstrom tongs. Some recklessly pick up the snakes with their bare hands and place them in the sack, the top of which is then tied with a knot. Venomous snakes may be pinned down by the neck and carefully picked up behind the head and placed in the bag tail first. Once the snake has been prevented from escaping, the angle hook or clamp can lift it into a bag held open by a circular frame made of a wire coat hanger or hoopstick without danger of being bitten. Snakes not handled seem to thrive much better in captivity. The diamondback is most widely distributed in the southeastern United States, where it favors swampy land, often resting in hollow tree trunks or under leaves. Its favorite prey is the cottontail rabbit, and where that species is plentiful the rattlesnake is likely to be found. It will also feed upon smaller rodents, but very rarely, if at all, upon birds.

So powerful is its venom that a rabbit dies within a minute or two after being bitten. A cautious feeder, a rattlesnake in captivity will spend quite a long time examining its dead prey, touching it again and again with the tip of its tongue before commencing to swallow it.

This species does not take well to captivity. Full-grown snakes caught in the wild may refuse to feed and, although they can go for very long periods of time with no food, they eventually die. They rattle constantly when people are present. Diamondback rattlesnakes raised in captivity from birth fare much better, feeding freely, and showing far fewer signs of nervousness in the presence of keepers. They may produce more than a dozen living young which feed mostly upon small rodents. The young grow rapidly, reaching maturity in two years, at which time the tail buttons that they were born with have developed into full rattles.

The western diamondback rattlesnake (*C. atrox*), a close relative of the above-mentioned form, is also large, irritable, and dangerous, but it takes much more readily to captivity, feeding well on rabbits, rats, guinea pigs, and birds. Nevertheless, it rarely "tames," rattles at any disturbance, and strikes repeatedly at its keepers.

When encountered in the wild, the prairie rattlesnake (*C. viridis*) coils at once and often strikes so vigorously that its entire body may actually be thrown forward by the momentum. After a short period of captivity, this snake seems not to be disturbed, rarely rattles, and feeds promptly on small rodents and birds.

Because this snake is often found in the same vicinity as prairie dogs, and often, when alarmed, will seek refuge in the prairie dog's burrow, it was long believed that the two species had some kind of affinity. This, of course, has no basis in fact. If anything, the two are mortal enemies, the snake gliding into the prairie dog's burrow in search of food. Though a full-grown prairie dog is too large for the

The prairie rattlesnake (*Crotalus viridis viridis*) averages from 3 to 4 feet in length and occurs in dry grassland and rocky hills from South Dakota, Nebraska, and Kansas north into southern Canada, south into northern Mexico. (*Photo: Roy Pinney*)

snake, the young mammals are just the right size and make up many of the snake's meals.

The unique coloration of the tiger rattlesnake (*C. tigris*) has led to this snake's being named after one of the most feared of animals. Relatively inoffensive, it inhabits the rocky foothills of the mountain ranges of southern Arizona and the adjacent desert areas.

The horned rattlesnake (*C. cerastes*) is also known as the sidewinder because of its unique means of locomotion. If in no hurry, the sidewinder moves forward like most other snakes, but if it is trying to move rapidly in its usual habitat of loose desert sand, it throws its body forward in a series of sidewise loopings so that the trail looks like a series of *J*'s lying parallel to one another and moving in an oblique direction. Mostly nocturnal, its presence is often shown only by these peculiar tracks. The horns that are hinged to the head, and fold down over the eyes when a slight pressure is exerted, are to protect the eyes when the snake is pursuing prey underground.

The six subspecies of the tropical rattlesnake found south of the United States are greatly feared and justly so. Their venom is as potent as that of puff adder and cobra venom combined! They are distributed from the southeastern part of Mexico through Central America, and eastern South America from northern Colombia to northern Argentina.

The cascabel (*C. durissus terrificus*) has a venom that is extremely toxic; 75 per cent of all untreated adults bitten are expected to die. With prompt antivenin treatment, the fatality rate drops to less than 10 per cent. The venom produces minor local symptoms but very grave systemic effects. These include blindness, paralysis of the neck muscles, cessation of breathing and heartbeat, and finally death.

This venom does not appear to form adequate antibodies in horses, so that enormous amounts of antivenin are needed to counteract the effects of the bite of a snake of average dimensions. Ten ampoules (100 ml.) would appear to be an average initial dose, and twenty or more may be used.

The rattle consists of horny interlocking links which grow from the end of the tail. Each snake is born with a single button and is incapable of producing sound until it has acquired a new segment. Each time the snake sheds its skin a new segment is added to the rattle. Snakes shed once or twice a year on the average, but the rattle cannot be used to estimate the snake's age with any accuracy—they often break off and an old snake may have a short rattle.

Hunters and fishermen: *Do not expect a rattlesnake to rattle and so warn you of his presence!* Very often they are too sluggish to respond to the close approach of a human—usually only rattling when very much disturbed. They will not attack, and you are safe if you just avoid them. The snake you see is not the one to fear—it's the one you *don't* see that you might step on or put your hand on. Rattlers can strike as much as one third of their length. They are reluctant to bite if it can be avoided. All poisonous snakes depend on their venom to obtain their food. Without it they would starve to death.

Like all snakes, rattlers are dependent on animal prey. They feed largely on rodents—rats and mice—and their extinction would be worse than regrettable. For every rattlesnake that is killed, dozens of rats, mice, ground squirrels, gophers, take a new lease on life and increase their work of destruction—of crops, installations, even the eggs of game birds, to say nothing of some very deadly diseases they are known to carry. Rattlesnake hunts or roundups bent on exterminating them in given areas are to be deplored. Rattlers have never been a serious menace to human life, and they should be left undisturbed in undeveloped regions. There are no reliable statistics available on snakebite in the United States, but it is estimated that no more than twelve die. No doubt these could be saved with proper treatment. Bee and wasp stings take a far greater toll in the course of a year.

Especially through the medium of the Western movie, it has become common nowadays to use "rattlesnake" and "sidewinder" as terms of opprobrium—a practice which merely displays vast ignorance of the facts concerning these honorable animals—animals which are doing their good work so thoroughly as to make anyone proud that they, the rattlesnakes, are truly American.

SEA SNAKES

Sea serpents have been sighted in great numbers off the coasts of southern Asia and Australia. Millions of them are at this moment plying the Pacific waters of Mexico right up into the Gulf of California.

There has been no sudden hatching of giant deep-sea monsters set loose upon the world to terrorize mankind. These rather small, usually inoffensive creatures have been known to scientists, commercial fishermen, and gourmets for some time—sea snakes.

Ancient legends and modern tales would have us believe in the existence of truly enormous, though curiously elusive, deep-water "serpents." Many reputable scientific expeditions have gone out in search of these fascinating creatures, making use of sophisticated tracking equipment in an attempt to locate the notorious monster of Loch Ness.

Whether or not giant sea serpents exist outside the mind of man, we know that they cannot be members of the subfamilies of sea snakes, Hydrophiinae and Laticaudinae. Though sea snakes are among the most venomous of all vertebrates, their average adult length of 4 to 6 feet, and maximum length (in a few species) of about 9 feet, falls far short of legend.

There are probably more sea snakes in the world than any other kind of snake, yet they are the least known of reptiles. Only very recently have scientists been able to prove or disprove some of the amazing stories built up around this unique group of serpents.

There are more than fifty different species of sea snakes and almost all are extremely venomous. Their venom is from ten to forty times as toxic as that of the cobra. Some species are many times more poisonous than any known land snake. The bite is itself relatively painless but death by convulsions, respiratory failure, and paralysis may follow. No antivenin exists for many species of sea snakes.

The overall body form of most sea snakes does not differ greatly from that of land snakes. The graceful rhythmic movements of sea snakes shows that this basic design is quite suitable for sea duty. But interesting evolutionary adaptations have occurred and a closer look reveals many peculiarities.

Perhaps the most obvious adaptation of sea snakes is their flat-

Close-up of a sea snake's body showing compressed adaptation for swimming and flattened oarlike tail, which is used as a scull. (*Photo: William A. Dunson*)

tened, oarlike or rudderlike tail which they use for propulsion and steering. The nostrils are set forward instead of on either side of the snake's head and each is equipped with a valvelike flap to prevent intake of sea water. The ventral or belly plates, which are large and used for traction by land snakes, are of no use in the water and are therefore greatly reduced in size. A special salt-excreting gland makes it possible for sea snakes to drink sea water. A controllable heartbeat and lungs which are fully three quarters as long as the snake itself allow these snakes to stay submerged for as long as two hours, depending on water temperature and the snake's activity.

All sea snakes are tropical and prefer warm seas. Most occur in the waters off India, Southeast Asia, Indonesia, and Australia, but members of the genus *Pelamis* are much more wide-ranging. One species, the yellow-bellied sea snake (*Pelamis platurus*), is the most widespread venomous snake in the world, indeed the most widely distributed of all snakes. Its range extends from southern Siberia to the coasts of New Zealand and Tasmania, from Africa's Cape of Good Hope to American Pacific waters. Its wide dispersal is undoubtedly related to its ability, unique among sea snakes, to live on the surface of the open sea.

There are no sea snakes in the Atlantic or Mediterranean. The intolerably cold water of the Atlantic seems to be the single most important reason for its absence there. The Mediterranean is extremely salty and has a small and unsuitable population of potential prey for the snakes. Then, too, the formation of impassable geographical barriers and subsequent isolation of the Mediterranean Sea during the Cenozoic effectively precluded the possibility of future colonization by sea snakes in this area. Sea snakes could not have established a foothold in the Mediterranean before this time since they did not appear till after the Cenozoic.

Although sea snakes have not established a breeding population in the Atlantic, they *are* found in great numbers along the Pacific coasts of Mexico and Central America. Naturalists are therefore on the lookout for evidence of sea snake entry via the Panama Canal, which could result in dire consequences to Caribbean tourism and marine fauna (resorts in some areas of the Philippines have placed nets around bathing beaches in an effort to keep out the sea snakes). George V. Pickwell proposes that the overall likelihood of this is small. He maintains that the structure of the Panama Canal itself may be responsible for the snakes' inability to enter. The locks at each end and the high-level portion of the canal are filled with fresh water. Pickwell contends that the sea snake senses the abrupt change in salinity and the subsequent reduction of suitable prey. In addition, the snake seems to be a passive traveler and usually swims with the currents rather than against them. In the canal, water flows downward from the locks toward the ocean.

However slim the chance for breeding may be, the idea of sea snake entry into the Caribbean excites the public imagination. The threat of death from snakebite could be a powerful economic force in the tourist industry at Caribbean beaches. The construction of a sea-level canal through Panama has been proposed. Sea snake entry into the Caribbean would then be high on the list of enormous and unpredictable ecological problems that would inevitably result.

The life of sea snakes is still not well known, but many fascinating pieces of information have recently come to light. The yellow-bellied sea snake is the only known species of sea snake that feeds at the surface of the water. The rest capture their prey on or near the bottom in relatively shallow water (150 feet or less), though some may dive as deep as 500 feet, twice the maximum depth possible for a man holding his breath. Sea snakes differ widely in their swimming and diving ability; some species apparently conserve energy and avoid predation by remaining quiet on the bottom for considerable periods.

There appears to be a strong tendency toward feeding specialization, particularly where numerous species occur together. But most sea snakes prey on fish, which they capture laterally. Once the fish is caught, the snake "walks" to its head with its jaws and then swallows it whole. Their curved, sharp teeth help them grasp and manipulate the prey. Small victims are quickly swallowed head first, larger victims require the use of venom from their fixed, hollow fangs in the front of the upper jaw.

John E. McCosker has made a particular study of the feeding behavior of sea snakes and suggests that their highly toxic venom functions more as a feeding adaptation than as a defense mechanism.

The inability of sea snakes to overcome their faster-swimming and more maneuverable prey has required behavioral strategies that include: nocturnal feeding on diurnally active fishes and, conversely, diurnal feeding on nocturnal fishes; surface feeding among accumulated surface drift and on fishes living in association with pelagic medusae; specialization to feed only on fish eggs; and feeding on fossorial fishes and, in particular, eels.

Eels are often mistaken for sea snakes. Some eels resemble sea snakes so much that they are called "snake eels." Pickwell has had people describe sea snakes they had seen during dives in an area where sea snakes are known not to occur. Upon closer questioning, the animal could usually be identified as an eel. Eels are not venomous and have no fangs. They have a pointed (not paddlelike) tail, fins (sometimes hard to see), a gill pouch in the neck area, and are visibly smooth, slippery, and slimy due to the usual fish coating of mucous which sea snakes do not have.

Examples of some feeding specialists include *Microcephalophis gracilis,* a thin, small-headed snake which grows to about 5 feet in length and is one of the most venomous of sea snakes. It feeds on fish eggs and has been seen with its head stuck in the sand and body waving in the current for perhaps forty minutes, presumably feeding on eggs (note that this highly venomous snake does not use its venom for killing prey since it feeds entirely on eggs). The heavy-bodied olive snake (*Aipysurus laevis*), which reaches a length of 6 feet, cannot catch free-swimming fishes and must corner them in a hole or crevice (this is one of the snakes for which no antivenin exists).

Aside from man, the one universal predator, there are few animals which attack or regularly feed upon sea snakes. Although sea snakes, along with almost any edible or inedible thing in the sea, have been found in the stomachs of sharks, they are not believed to be regular predators. Teleost fish, including the moray eel, catfish, large grouper, and blue cod, may occasionally feed upon sea snakes. Many fish will not eat sea snakes, for reasons which are not fully understood, but it is known that these snakes, eaten whole, are capable of inflicting fatally poisonous bites on the stomach walls of predatory fish. Incredibly, they may then actually escape through the dead fish's mouth.

The red-backed and white-breasted sea eagles are known to prey upon sea snakes. The snakes are caught as they surface for air and brought to land by the eagles, where they are killed by being dropped on the rocks. Other seabirds may occasionally prey upon sea snakes in this way; for example, a frigate bird was observed picking up a sea snake swimming at the surface and carrying it for a short distance.

For the yellow-bellied sea snake there is substantial evidence for only one kind of mortality factor and this is a physical one—that of being swept by currents onto the shore. Even heavier losses to the population may occur as snakes are carried by currents into areas of lethally cold water.

SUBMERGENCE

Sea snakes and file snakes commonly voluntarily submerge (or if on the surface, hold their breath) for periods of 5 to 30 minutes but may do so for up to about 1½ to 2 hours. There is a great variability in submergence time, which is reduced by activity and increased temperature. Submergence times were measured by H. Heatwole in New South Wales, Australia, under three major types of conditions—in the field, in laboratory containers, and in a respirometer. In addition, one series of measurements was made in a municipal swimming pool.

Field measurements were made by underwater observations of snakes by snorkeling or with the aid of scuba equipment until an individual surfaced to breathe. With an underwater stopwatch, the snake was timed until its next surfacing; its activity in the interim was noted. On occasions, unsolicited attention by sharks or exhaustion of scuba air supply necessitated breaking off observations before a snake had resurfaced.

Breathing could be detected visually by the opening and closing of the nostril valves, or by expansion and contraction of girth, and usually audibly by the sound of exhaled air.

With the exception of *Laticauda,* which breeds on land, marine snakes seldom leave the water. Except for the pelagic yellow-bellied species, these animals carry out most of their biological activities while submerged and often spend long periods of time on the bottom at considerable depths. Snakes which have been either foraging or resting on the bottom will swim nearly vertically to the surface, the momentum carrying their heads well above the water. One (often audible) exhalation is followed by an inhalation and an immediate return to the bottom, usually descending nearly vertically. Frequently exhalation begins 10 to 15 centimeters below the surface and bubbles can be seen streaming from the snake's nostrils during the last part of its ascent. Only rarely does a snake stay at the surface for a second or third breath, and then only for a few seconds. Under some conditions in nature many species of sea snakes will spend long periods of time floating at the surface. This has often been interpreted as "basking," though it may also occur at night. Snakes on the surface usually dive when approached and cannot be observed closely. Consequently, it is not known whether their breathing rhythm is similar to that of snakes at the water's surface in a laboratory aquarium. Greater metabolic demands of active snakes as compared to inactive ones tend to reduce the voluntary submergence time.

Some intriguing observations have been made on what might be called the migratory habits of sea snakes. William A. Dunson describes some sea snakes that move up into river mouths, continue into freshwater lakes, and remain there. Apparently the lower salinity of the water is not physiologically detrimental to them. Yellow-bellied sea snakes have been kept in fresh water for six months.

One of the most astounding observations ever recorded about sea snakes was made by W. P. Lowe in the Strait of Malacca. Near the island of Sumatra and the Malay Peninsula, while on a sea voyage, he saw a long line running parallel to the ship's course, about four or five miles distant. As the ship drew nearer to satisfy everyone's curiosity, they were amazed to find that it was composed of a solid mass of sea snakes thickly twisted together. They were orange-red and black, a massive, very poisonous, and rare variety known as *Astrotia stokesii*. Along this line there must have been millions, for it was about ten feet wide and some sixty miles long! Many people have seen snakes of this description but never in such massed formation.

Although sea snakes are dangerous, they are generally mild-mannered. In most instances they will not display aggressive behavior unless they are interfered with. When approached by humans, the snakes' reaction ranges from indifference to what might be termed "mild avoidance." This depends on the nearness of the man and his direction of travel. But, if provoked, the snake will attack. It is believed that it is only in these instances of self-defense that the snake will eject its venom.

Harold Heatwole notes that the aggressiveness of sea snakes is a subject upon which there has been much divergence of opinion but little careful systematic observation. Various authorities have used terms ranging from "vicious" and "ferocious" to "docile," "gentle," and "inoffensive." As with many other behavioral traits, temperament shows considerable interspecific differences.

A great number of animals will attempt to bite a molester when captured, cornered, or persistently disturbed. This is such a generalized defensive pattern that it is not surprising that many sea snakes employ it. It is an erroneous belief that the small-headed species cannot get a sufficient gape to cause a dangerous bite on a finger or other appendage.

As with their terrestrial counterparts, most sea snakes will immediately leave the scene when a human approaches. I am as skeptical of sea snake attacks as I am of the aggressive intent of land species. In my pursuit of sea snakes, none has ever turned the tables and attacked me. I have had several species attempt to bite the Pillstrom tongs I was using to capture them. Heatwole records a filmed experiment in which the snakes were deliberately molested to provoke attacks. In contrast to the slow, leisurely way a curious snake may approach a diver, perhaps attracted to the air bubbles emanating from the scuba equipment, an attacking snake moves with astonishing rapidity; the graceful undulations of ordinary locomotion give way to a rather jerky movement (perhaps simply a function of increased swimming speed) which gives the impression that the head is darting back and forth. The most characteristic feature of attacking snakes is their persistence. They chase fleeing divers for long distances and repeatedly return to the attack after being violently kicked with flippers or pushed aside by a spear gun or snake tongs. Escaping or fending off an attacking snake can be an exhausting experience, especially for the uninitiated. In one instance, a snake bit the diver (protected by a wet suit) four times before giving up the attack.

The behavioral differences between a curious snake and an attacking one are striking; the latter leaves no doubt in the mind of the recipient as to the aggressive nature of the action. According to Heatwole, once one has experienced or seen an attack, it is subsequently easy to distinguish between the approaches of curious and aggressive snakes.

The best way to avoid attack is not to molest snakes and, if approached, to refrain from vigorous activity, especially striking the animal. Attacks can sometimes be diverted by dropping a rope in front of an attacking snake. Wet suits are good protection against most species. Any form of recklessness or exhibitionism in handling sea snakes constitutes unwarranted risk to the diver and his underwater companions and should be avoided. On the whole, swimmers and divers are less endangered by sea snakes than waders who may step on them in muddy waters.

Sea snakes constitute a threat to the native fishermen of Southeast Asia. Most bites occur when the fishermen are wading in muddy shallows or when they are sorting their catch from nets, as sea snakes are frequently taken along with the fish. The response of native fishermen to the snake varies depending on the local tradition and superstition of each area. In the Gulf of Panama, shrimp fishermen routinely decapitate the yellow-bellied sea snake, while in other regions they are regarded with complete indifference.

The Philippines are probably one of the richest fishing grounds for sea snakes in the world. Originally started in 1934 by the Japanese, who taught the local fishermen how to catch and prepare them for commercial use, the industry is overexploited. Emmanuel Y. Punay, general manager of the Sea Snakes Company of the Philippines in Manila, stresses the urgent need for implementation of a plan for conservation so that the fishery can continue on a sustained-yield basis.

Sea snakes are often gathered by hand. The body and the neck are grabbed and the snakes are put in a sack. The *Laticauda* species are inoffensive and tend to shy away from a capturing hand. Many fishermen even claim that "they don't bite." However, they are quite capable of striking if roughly handled or disturbed by sudden temperature changes. Snake divers often bundle as many as seven specimens together with bands of rubber cut from discarded motorcycle tubes, an efficient though risky procedure that snakes respond to by striking. While the bites are rarely fatal, they are extremely painful. *Hydrophis belcheri,* which, according to Punay, has a dangerous bite and puts up a formidable fight, is most frequently found in the open sea, above coral reefs. Baitfish, employed as chum, attract them in droves; the fishermen wait for the right moment, then dive and capture the snakes by hand. Baited scoop nets are also used as traps; they are set on ledges 30–40 feet below the surface. A skillful diver can seize two or three sea snakes in each hand, repeating this performance a dozen times a day (or night). Another effective though tiring method is patrol diving; likely areas are cautiously patrolled by boats until a snake is spotted breathing near the surface. The hunters—for such is their function—then dive, their speed increased by weights, and overtaking the fleeing snake, grab it. With luck, they pounce on still others feeding at the bottom.

Fishermen occasionally catch sea snakes on their hooks and lines, *basnigs* (bag nets), and trawls. Whenever fishermen operate near coral reefs and rocky shelves, they often catch sea snakes which are after the fish that the men are catching.

Laticauda species can generally be found under overhanging ledges or inside islet caves with underwater entrances. Divers strap underwater flashlights to one arm to search these areas. *L. colubrina* is often easier to gather since it coils on top of rocks on islets where conditions are cool and damp. The *Hydrophis* are mostly gathered by chumming in the open sea above coral reefs.

Over the ages and all over the world, peoples of both past and present have considered the flesh of snakes to have magical properties, serving as medicine or, in the case of a Manila restaurant, Mariposa de la Vida (Butterfly of Life), as an aphrodisiac. The guest may select a sea snake from the management's aquarium and have an "exotic" dish prepared from it, to be served at his table. Perhaps not today, but not too very long ago, some customers would order a live specimen, slit its throat, and drink the blood. Following this rather outré apéritif, the still-wriggling snake was diced and eaten raw, with soy sauce.

For the true gourmet, there is an entree called Sea Snake Adobo. The sliced meat is soaked in vinegar, then in soy sauce mixed with a combination of pimento and garlic, for fifteen minutes. The mixture is then boiled in a solution of soda for a half hour, after which it is drained, fried, and garnished with pickles, onions, and tomatoes *al gusto*. An alleged aphrodisiac, though to the weak of stomach more likely an emetic, the gall bladder is chugalugged with a glass of wine. In the case of a nondrinker, three dried gall bladders may be boiled in coffee and then consumed.

VENOMOUS NONVENOMOUS SNAKES

Almost all of the Colubridae, with 1,518 species recognized, are thought to be nonvenomous except for about sixteen species. Of the latter, the boomslang and bird snake of Africa are known to be very dangerous. But lately herpetologists have been looking into the possibility that a few so-called harmless snakes may be venomous. There are no recorded deaths from such snakes but the alarming symptoms from a few cases are causing concern. Some people may be allergic to the snake saliva.

The common hognose snake has always been considered a clown of the reptile world because of its extraordinary behavior. When approached and disturbed, it often inflates its body with air, makes a hissing sound, goes into convulsions, turns over on its back, opens its mouth with the tongue hanging out, and looks very dead. Put it back on its belly and it will immediately turn over on its back again. When the apparent danger seems gone, it will once again right itself and crawl away.

Since the biochemistry of snake venoms involves complex poisons, the saliva of some snakes formerly regarded as harmless may contain a toxic substance which may produce uncomfortable reactions from a bite. Bites from the hognose snake, the garter snake, and a colubrid from Japan known as *yamakagashi,* which is often used as food, have been known in rare instances to cause hand swelling and severe headaches accompanied by internal bleeding.

It is not certain at this time what these and other nonvenomous snakes actually have that produces such reactions, but it would be wise to be cautious, and if bitten, be aware of the possibility of a local infection that may require medical scrutiny. Even more important, however, is not to become paranoid about snakes.

IMPORTANT VENOMOUS SNAKES OF THE WORLD

Family and type of fangs	Common names	Type of venom	Distribution	Remarks
Colubridae; a few venomous sp.; rear, immovable, grooved	Colubrids	Mostly mild	Warm parts of both hemispheres	Over 1,500 species
Examples:	Boomslang	Hemorrhagin	South Africa	Arboreal, timid
	Bird snake	Hemorrhagin	Tropical Africa	Inflates neck
Elapidae; front, immovable grooved	Elapids	Predominantly neurotoxin	Mostly in Old World	Over 150 species; very poisonous
Examples:	Cobras	Mostly neurotoxin	Africa, India, Asia, Philippines, Celebes	Spitting Cobra in Africa aims at eyes
	Kraits	Strong neurotoxin	India, S.E. Asia, East Indies	Sluggish, often buried in dust
	Mambas	Neurotoxin	Tropical W. Africa	Arboreal
	Blacksnake	Neurotoxin	Australia	Large snake
	Copperhead	Neurotoxin	Australia, Tasmania, Solomons	Damp environment
	Brown snake	Neurotoxin	Australia, New Guinea	Slender

Family and type of fangs	Common names	Type of venom	Distribution	Remarks
	Tiger snake	Strong neurotoxin	Australia	Dry environment; aggressive; very dangerous
	Death adder	Neurotoxin	Australia, New Guinea	Sandy terrain
	Coral snakes	Neurotoxin	U.S., tropical America	About 26 species, 2 in s. U.S.
Hydrophidae; front, immovable, hollow	Sea snakes	Some mild; others very toxic	Tropical, Indian & Pacific Oceans	Gentle; rudderlike tail; over 50 species
Viperidae; front, movable, hollow	True vipers	Predominantly hematoxin	Entirely in Old World	About 50 species
Examples:	European viper	Hematoxin	Europe (rare), N. Africa, Near East	Dry rocky country
	Russell's viper	Hematoxin	S.E. Asia, Java, Sumatra	Mostly open terrain; deadly
	Sand vipers	Hematoxin	N. Sahara	Buried in sand
	Puff adder	Hematoxin	Arabia, Africa	Open terrain; sluggish
	Gaboon viper	Neurotoxin and hematoxin	Tropical W. Africa	Forests; deadly

Family and type of fangs	Common names	Type of venom	Distribution	Remarks
	Rhinoceros viper	Hematoxin	Tropical Africa	Wet forests
Crotalidae; front, movable, hollow	Pit vipers	Predominantly hematoxin	Old and New Worlds; none in Africa	Over 80 species; pit between eye and nostril
Examples:	Rattlesnakes	Predominantly hematoxin	N., Central & S. America	South American form neurotoxic
	Bushmaster	Hematoxin	Central & S. America	Large; in wet forests
	Fer-de-lance	Hematoxin	Found only on Martinique, Fr. West Indies	Common on plantations
	Palm vipers	Hematoxin (?)	S. Mexico, Central and S. America	Arboreal; small, greenish; bite face
	Copperhead	Hematoxin	United States	Dry stony terrain
	Water moccasin	Hematoxin	Southeast U.S. to Texas	Swamps
	Asiatic pit vipers	Hematoxin	S.E. Asia, Formosa	Most arboreal

Source: *Manual of Tropical Medicine,* Military Medical Manuals, National Research Council.

SNAKEBITE THERAPY

With proper first aid and subsequent medical treatment, a victim of venomous snakebite is in less danger of losing his life than one might think. About 45,000 Americans are bitten by snakes yearly, but only 8,000 of these bites are by poisonous snakes and less than 0.2 per cent of poisonous bites are fatal. Young children and elderly people account for a large percentage of the dozen or so yearly deaths by snake poisoning in this country.

Some knowledge of the habits of venomous snakes and a few simple precautions will reduce your chances of being bitten. Consider first that 94 per cent of all snakebites in the United States occur during the warm months between April and October. When the temperature reaches 80 to 90 degrees, as it does often during the peak snakebite months of July and August, snakes are most active and the chances of an encounter between man and snake are increased. At or below 40 degrees, snakes, like all cold-blooded reptiles, become immobile and are rarely seen. The incidence of snakebite is highest in the South and Southwest, but venomous snakes are found in all states except Alaska, Hawaii, and Maine.

If you or a friend are bitten by a snake, there is no time to indulge in emotional or hysterical behavior. Chances are that the snake is not venomous and that, even if it is, there has been little or no venom injected into the wound: 27 per cent of poisonous snakebites involve no venom and 37 per cent involve ineffectual amounts.

In the United States, most venomous bites are caused by members of the pit viper family (Crotalidae), so called because of the pit between eye and nostril on either side of the snake's head; a pair of large fangs descend from the upper jaw. This family includes the copperhead and timber rattler, the diamondback rattlers, and the cottonmouth or water moccasin. Bites by coral snakes (Elapidae) are fortunately much less common, but are cause for concern.

Both families of venomous snakes have evolved a highly efficient mechanism for biting and injecting venom under pressure through hollow fangs. The venom originates in a modified salivary gland above the fangs, which are always needle sharp due to continual replacement. Snake venom is a complex substance which produces many and varied effects: no venom has only one action.

The most dramatic manifestation of pit viper venom is swelling and discoloration around the wound due to local tissue damage. This is caused by the action of digestive enzymes; venom is used by these snakes to kill and partially digest their prey—a useful enough function in animals which do not chew. But tissue damage is not the most dangerous action of venom. For example, the venom of the Mojave rattlesnake (*Crotalus scutulatus*) causes little tissue damage; yet it is otherwise the most lethal of North American rattlesnake venoms. Other serious effects include internal hemorrhaging, an increase or decrease in the blood's ability to clot, and, in the case of coral snake venoms, neurotoxic effects. It is important to realize that rattlesnake venom, while about 7,000 times less deadly than botulinus toxin (the most potent toxin known) is still some 50,000 times more toxic than cyanide.

It is clear that immediate action should be taken if so dangerous a substance is injected into the body. But the problem of what constitutes proper first aid for snakebite is a controversial one and still not completely resolved.

Many years ago, longer than I care to recall, I was collecting along the canal that skirts the Forty-mile Bend, a detour from the Tamiami Trial across the Everglades in Florida. I was frantically summoned by an attendant of a gas station down the road. where I had made a brief stop. He knew that I was interested in snakes and regarded me as an expert. A fisherman had been bitten on the hand by a moccasin and would I help him? I would and did, following the first-aid procedures taught at the time by the Boy Scouts. Someone had already tied a tourniquet around the wrist of the swollen palm. I made a gesture of sterilizing a razor blade by heating it with the flame of a lighted match. Heroically I made a half dozen crisscross cuts around the bite. The sight of blood doesn't sicken me, particularly if it is someone else's. I kneaded the area to induce a greater flow of blood and used a suction device at the incisions. Finally the victim's buddies arrived and he was taken to a Miami hospital.

Now, decades later, if that individual is still alive, he probably has some stiff fingers that he attributes to the snakebite. Actually, the blame belongs to the idiot who valiantly tried to be helpful. I am glad he doesn't know who I am!

The technique I used on the fisherman is no longer recommended —it is not very effective in removing venom from the wound and there is danger of cutting blood vessels or tendons. But the man's fate could have been worse! Consider the following two letters written to a prominent authority on snakebite poisoning:

Dear Doctor:

Please try this magic cure for snakebite.

Sprinkle cold water on the face of the victim and shout in a commanding tone thrice: "Get up! It is the command of T. C. Ramachander Rao!"

I hope this will cure the boy. It has cured thousands in India.

Dear Doctor:

Do you know about toad pee? This is the best cure for all snakebite. Catch a toad and squeeze his pee into the wound, then kill the toad and leave wound soaked with pee; this will kill the snakebite. My grandfather used to be bit by lots of snakes and never died because of this treatment.

There are scores of equally creative folk remedies, most of which have been carefully evaluated and found to be useless.

Prone to collecting snakes on my worldwide travels, including venomous bushmasters, fer-de-lances, mambas, cobras, coral snakes, rattlesnakes, etc., I was much concerned about what to do in case of a bite. I wrote to authorities around the world. Some recommended cryotherapy, in which the bitten area is immersed in or packed with ice; others sponsored incision, excision, and/or injection of antivenin into the bite area.

Since there is such a considerable diversity of opinion, professional and otherwise, about what constitutes proper venomous snakebite therapy, I have sometimes felt that if I were bitten I would die from indecision as I reviewed the different steps dictated by the various treatments. But, after considerable research, I have decided to follow faithfully the procedures recommended by Dr. Findlay E. Russell, professor of physiology, neurology, and biology at the University of Southern California, director of the Laboratory of Neurological Research, Los Angeles County / U.S.C. School of Medicine, and director of the Toxicology Laboratory, Portal, Arizona. Dr. Russell (to whom the two previously quoted folk-remedy letters were sent) has had wide experience and notable success in the treatment of venomous snakebite. He and his colleagues have written authoritatively on the subject, and their advice, reduced to a concise form for emergency purposes, is given below.

A general first-aid policy of minimal intervention seems best. Apply a light tourniquet above the wound; loosen it for 90 seconds every 10 minutes. If the snake is identified as a pit viper and the bite is *not* on the hands, fingers, or toes, make quarter-inch-long superficial incisions through the fang marks immediately and apply suction. But if 30 minutes or more have passed since the bite or if the snake is an elapid (coral snakes, cobras, etc.), this procedure is practically useless.

Keep the victim calm and rested—no walking or other movement and no alcohol. Many of the symptoms of venomous snakebite, such as weakness, faintness, sweating, nausea, and even shock, may be caused solely by the emotional reaction of the victim. Transport the patient quickly and quietly to the hospital.

The severity of a snakebite depends on the size and age of the individual, amount of venom injected, and toxic potency of the venom. The method of "grading" bites on the basis of selected symptoms and signs has been found to be inadequate. A doctor's judgment of a bite as minimal, moderate, or severe, taking into account *all* clinical manifestations and relevant tests, is an important first step in his decision concerning how much of the right kind of antivenin to administer. In severe cases more than 20 vials may be needed.

Antivenin is most effective if given soon after the bite, but is helpful to the victim at any time. The antivenin used to neutralize pit viper venoms (Antivenin Crotalidae Polyvalent) is a horse serum. Many people are violently allergic to this and must be given powerful counteractive drugs. Thus, antivenin should be given only in a hospital setting. Rabbit- or goat-prepared antivenin, which, unlike the horse serum, is species-specific, may be available for those with severe allergies to horse serum. For coral snakes or exotic foreign snakes, specific antivenins are stocked by some hospitals and by large zoos.

Dr. Findlay E. Russell with his associates, Dr. Albert Picchioni, Dr. Richard W. Carlson, Dr. Jack Wainschel, and Dr. Arthur H.

Osborne, have had experience with approximately 700 cases of snake-venom poisoning. And here is what they have recommended, reduced to a concise form for emergency purposes:

To be effective, treatment must be instituted immediately. Bear in mind *all* clinical manifestations, including changes in the blood cells and blood chemistry, deficiencies in neuromuscular transmission, changes in motor and sensory function, and the like.

MANAGEMENT OF SNAKE-VENOM POISONING

I. FIRST-AID MEASURES

A. Constriction Band, Incisions, and Suction

1. If patient is seen within 30 minutes of bite, and there is evidence of envenomation, place constriction band 5–10 cm. proximal or above first joint proximal to bite. Band should be tight enough to occlude lymph flow but not to impede venous or arterial circulation.
2. Incise through fang marks. Incision should be no more than 1 cm. long and no deeper than 3 mm. Incisions are of no value if delayed more than 30 minutes.
3. Apply suction cup.
4. Do not make cuts anywhere except through fang marks.

B. Immobilization and Rest

1. Immobilize affected part and place in a physiological or normal position.
2. Keep patient at rest and give reassurance.
3. Under no conditions should the part be placed in ice, the bite area excised, or surgical measure performed unless approved by the Admitting Room Director in hospital.
4. Give liquid or soft diet, if tolerated.
5. Maintain patent airway.
6. Administer oxygen or apply positive-pressure breathing as needed.
7. Splint injured extremity in loose cast in physiological position below heart level.
8. Antihistamines or corticosteroids may be administered to treat allergic reactions to antivenin or venom. Do not

use corticosteroids during acute phase of poisoning except for shock or severe allergic reaction.

C. Follow-up Care

1. Cleanse and cover wound with sterile dressing.
2. Debridement (removal of foreign matter and devitalized tissue around wound) should be performed, if necessary, on third to tenth day. Elevate slightly after fourth day.
3. Soak part for at least 15 minutes 3 times daily in 1:20 Aluminum Acetate Solution, U.S.P. (Burow's Solution). Bubble oxygen through solution at least once a day.
4. Paint wound once daily following debridement with an aqueous dye solution containing brilliant green 1:400, gentian violet 1:400, and acriflavine 1:1,000. Apply antimicrobial cream at bedtime.
5. Evaluate need for physical therapy on third or fourth day; begin active exercise immediately.

On admission to the hospital the following tests should be carried out immediately: typing and cross-matching; bleeding, clotting, and clot retraction times; complete blood cell count; hematocrit determination; platelet count; and urinalysis. Red blood cell indices, sedimentation rate, prothrombin time, arterial blood gas measurements, and determinations of sodium, potassium, and chloride may be needed. In severe poisonings, an electrocardiogram is indicated. Serum protein levels, fibrinogen titer, partial thromboplastin time, and renal function tests are often useful. In severe envenomation the hematocrit, blood count, hemoglobin concentration, and platelet count should be carried out several times for the first few days, and all urine samples should be examined, particularly for red blood cells.

II. MEDICAL TREATMENT

A. Antivenin

1. Test for serum sensitivity by means of conjunctiva or skin test (see brochure in antivenin kit). If sensitivity test is positive, get consultation before administering antivenin.
2. Antivenin (Crotalidae) Polyvalent (produced by Wyeth Laboratories) is the antitoxin of choice in all North

American crotalid bites. Administer antivenin intra-
venously in continuous saline drip, if possible, and in all
cases of shock. 3–20 vials of antivenin may be necessary
during the first 6 hours.

3. If it is necessary to administer antivenin intramuscularly,
   give in buttocks. Do not inject antivenin i.m. if it can be
   given i.v.
4. Never inject antivenin into a toe or finger.
5. Measure circumference of extremity 10–20 cm. proximal
   to bite and at a second point proximal to that every 15
   minutes, as one guide to antivenin administration.
6. Have available the following items: tourniquet, oxygen,
   Adrenalin, antishock drugs, tracheostomy equipment, and
   positive-pressure breathing apparatus.

B. Supportive Measures

1. Administer broad-spectrum antimicrobial agent if there is
   severe tissue involvement.
2. Administer appropriate antitetanus agent (antitoxin/
   toxoid).
3. Administer plasma, albumin, whole blood, or platelets,
   as indicated.
4. Aspirin or codeine may be given for pain.
5. Limit administration of i.v. fluids during period of acute
   edema.
6. Mild sedation may be indicated in all severe bites and
   when respiratory depression is not a problem.

Men Versus Snakes

SNAKE WORSHIP

While man's attitude toward the snake has been remarkably ambivalent over the centuries—hate and revulsion vs. love and veneration—there is no question that serpent worship at one time was widespread, and does indeed still exist today. This duality of feeling includes other opposites, as, for example, magic and healing vs. danger and death, graphically symbolized in the caduceus, emblem of the medical profession, with its intertwined serpents.

Wonder and awe, in sufficient intensity, are but a step from veneration, and it is not difficult to see why the serpent's many remarkable qualities elevated its image to that of a deity. Nicholas P. Christy, M.D., who conducted studies on the contiguous areas of ophiaphobia and ophiolatry—the self-contradictory yet overlapping fear-and-worship of snakes, made note of "the characteristic shedding of the skin which has been thought of as the symbol of renewal, and by extension, of immortality [of the snake]"; also "the capacity to renew its fangs so that there is always a new and sharp poison fang in the anterior part of the maxilla." These are phenomena which the ancients observed, surely with a mixture of fear and wonder. Because of this strange ability to slough off its skin and emerge anew, the ancient Mesopotamians believed it immortal.

Other observed factual characteristics, including the fixed, unblinking stare (leading to the myth that a snake can charm or hypnotize its prey) and its ability to remain absolutely immobile, contributed to its image, both alive and in symbolic form, as worthy of worship. It was worshipped in ancient times as a regenerative power, as a solar deity, a phallic deity, a god of evil, and a god of death.

The Ophites, a Gnostic sect of the second century A.D., worshipped the serpent of Eden for attempting to bestow upon Adam and Eve the mysterious knowledge withheld from them by Jehovah.

The serpent was the symbol of Satan, the Egyptian god Ra, and Apollo, the Greek god whose temple was called Pytho, after the legendary serpent Python, which he, as a child, was said to have slain. Among Greek Dionysiac cults, the serpent as a symbol represented fertility and wisdom. It is said that in Rome, during the Empire period, snakes were kept in special enclosures within each temple. Vestal virgins were charged with the care of the serpents. If one of them proffered food and it was rejected, this was taken as proof that the attendant no longer was a virgin, and she suffered the death penalty.

The Indians, Siamese, and Burmese venerated the snake as a semi-god and semi-demon. The worship of Krishna, and eventually Vishnu, was incorporated with the beliefs of primitive snake cults. Buddha, according to legend, received the true Buddhism from what was regarded as the king of serpents—presumably the king cobra. In this faith, the regenerative powers of the snake were at times revered, according to the same legend.

Amulets and religious emblems with representations of snakes were highly esteemed in ancient Egypt and appear in ethnological studies of peoples in all quarters of the globe. One of the most notable examples is that of the plumed serpent, symbol of Quetzalcoatl, ancient god and legendary ruler of the Toltecs. The Aztecs adopted Quetzalcoatl, linked him with their war god Huitzilopochtli, and Kukulcán, the Mayan equivalent, occupied Chichén Itzá, in the uncovered ruins of which, along with those of Uxmal, are to be seen the gigantic carved stone representations of stylized serpents, some adorned with rattles. The connection of the plumed serpent with snake worship is obvious. The gods themselves, however, predominate as legendary men, in both attributes and characteristics, rather than as serpentlike objects of veneration.

As a sacred personality the python has predominated in Africa. Many python huts or temples have been noted by observers. In Dahomey, the python has ranked high among gods, credited with powers of good, including those of influencing the weather in times of drought or flood. At one time, killing a python was punished as a capital offense. If one entered a hut, its presence was regarded as a good omen. In fact, the powerful yet relatively harmless (to hu-

The python represents the most sacred of African serpents. This may be due in part to its impressive size and relative harmlessness to humans. Python huts or temples were noted by many observers. One report describes python worship in Dahomey. "The snake is invoked in excessively wet, dry, or barren seasons, and on all occasions relating to government." Betrothed girls of the Murenda tribe near Sibasi in South Africa are doing the python dance, a ritual fertility invocation. (*Photo: Hamilton Wright/Photo-library Inc.*)

mans) qualities of the snake gave credence to its high deistic rank— that of a superhuman being, god of war, spirit of the water, patron of agriculture, and goddess of fertility.

Just as killing a python was forbidden in Africa, the king cobra enjoys similar protection in India. A fatal bite is considered a deistic punishment and goes untreated; thus the high fatality rate from such attacks. The cobra is regarded by many as the protector of a village, and therefore must not be molested.

An equivalent reverence toward snakes has been noted as connected with, though not as the central figure in, religions of various
American Indian tribes. L. M. Klauber, in his two-volume work
*Rattlesnakes: Their Habits, Life Histories, and Influence on Man-
kind,* citing numerous ethnologists and other investigators, describes
the propitiatory or protective attitudes and practices of Indian tribes
during the eighteenth and nineteenth centuries. Illness, various disas-
ters, and even death were feared if the taboo against killing a rattler
was broken. Should that happen, a pardon or a gift—often tobacco
—was given.

The teeth, rattles, oil, and flesh of a rattler were often highly
prized for supposed magical properties, but the killing had to be a
ritual one, according to the Cherokees, carried out by a priest. The
association with water and with lightning was frequent, in widely
separated areas. It is easy to see how the strike of a snake might be
connected with the speed and pattern of a lightning stroke. The
dichotomy involved in separating reverence from respect, and actual
worship from fear demanding propitiations, is difficult, if not impossible. But it is safe to make the following generalization: In remote
times, serpent worship was a widespread actuality. In more recent
times, such veneration has given way to a blend of respectful
animism and realistic basic caution—a broth stirred with the stick of
superstition.

SNAKES OF THE BIBLE

As mathematicians and physicists work to piece together a picture
of the future, men of other disciplines and sciences are having equal
success in reconstructing and recalling the past. The most dramatic
progress made by the latter group has included filling in the details
of man's early adventures as recorded in the Bible.

One fascinating aspect of this recovery of the past—until now not
made available to the general public—has been an identification to a
high degree of accuracy of the animal life that figured in the pastoral
and agricultural setting of the biblical world. Improved readings of
the basic texts in Hebrew, reinforced by a knowledge of the languages of the surrounding peoples—such as Ugaritic, Akkadian,
Sumerian, and Egyptian—now permit the reader to know with a
great measure of accuracy the fauna of those early days. Preserved

in the Bible is a detailed panorama of Near East animal life of millennia ago.

Genesis is remarkably close in some respects. It states that life first arose in the waters and then penetrated the land, a fact mirrored in our modern hypothesis that such animals as the lungfish, salamander, and lizards represent transitional phases between the fish and higher forms such as the mammals.

The snakes include the common name, Hebrew equivalent, and the binomial identification if known.

VIPER   (Adder)   Akshub   *Vipera palestina, Cerastes cerastes, Pseudocerastes fieldi, et al.*

"Dan shall be a serpent by the way, an adder in the path, that biteth the horse heels, so that his rider shall fall backward"
(Gen. 49:17)
"He shall suck the poison of asps: the viper's tongue shall slay him"   (Job 20:16)
"And when Paul had gathered a bundle of sticks, and laid them on the fire, there came a viper out of the heat, and fastened on his hand"   (Acts 28:3)

The snake referred to here is now thought to be the horned viper (*Cerastes cerastes*). The older books have this snake classified as *Cerastes hasselquistii,* a desert species with a very toxic venom. It is relatively small, about 12 to 18 inches long, and as pale and sandy as the desert it thrives in. Over each eye there is a sharp, upright spine which gives it the name of the horned or arrow snake. It hides in the sand, in depressions such as those made by the hooves of camels or horses, and if a man or an animal steps into such a hollow, the snake may strike. It is supposed to strike sometimes without provocation, and its venom has been said to kill in half an hour, making it as deadly as a cobra. This is believed to be the "asp" that killed Cleopatra.

There is also a representative of a closely allied genus of snakes in Israel. This is known as the false viper (*Pseudocerastes fieldi*), a small true desert species with valves inside its nostrils to seal them against the ultra-fine grains of sandstorms.

The word "viper" can refer to a large number of different members of the family Viperidae, all of which are venomous. The family is divided into a number of genera, one of which is *Vipera,* which is characterized by the presence of scales on the head that are of nearly the same size and type as those of the upper part of the body. The adder of Europe (*Vipera berus*) is a member of this genus, and ranges from England to Korea and Sakhalin. Closely related, but not to be confused with the horned viper (*Cerastes*), is the nose-horned viper (*Vipera ammodytes*). It measures less than 2 feet, and is characterized by a small horn arising from the tip of the snout. It lies low in the sand, often biting the heels of whatever mammal may trespass. The color is gray, giving it excellent camouflage. The Hebrew word for viper is *akshub,* or "coiling back," apparently derived from the characteristic posture of the animal. The bite is said to be extremely toxic. Another member of the same genus is the Palestine viper (*Vipera palestina*). This snake possesses a neck which distends in the same way that the cobra's does. It is green in color, marked obliquely with brown bands. The length varies from 3 to 5 feet. Its bite allegedly brings instant and almost painless death. For this reason it became a highly preferred method of suicide, and, were it available, would have been a much more likely candidate for Cleopatra's asp.

The name "adder" is an English equivalent of "viper," used for the viper of the British Isles.

ASP   (Cobra)   Pethen   *Naja haje*

The word "asp" is derived from the Greek *aspis,* which meant any poisonous snake. In Old English it could, at one time, denote any snake from the region of Egypt or North Africa. However, there is now little doubt that it denotes, in the English translations of the Bible, the Egyptian cobra (*Naja haje*), still another snake that has been named as the one that killed Cleopatra. It conceals itself in holes in walls and rocks, and has the power to expand its neck by raising its anterior ribs so as to dilate the front of its breast into the shape of a fat disk. When alarmed, it rises up with its neck spread out in this fashion and attacks when approached closely. In this pose it is depicted on ancient Egyptian monuments, where it represented immortality. The Egyptians looked upon it as a sacred creature.

Since it fed on the rodents which ate the Egyptians' crops, it seemed to the Egyptians to be a protector.

As one early historian put it:

One of the early Egyptian beliefs was that there first existed great silent darkness everywhere and that out of this great primordial night there evolved the world egg which eventually divided into the skies and the earth. Among the most common tradition is the one that ascribes to the Great World Serpent the warming and hatching of the egg, a phenomenon that has been commonly illustrated. (Henry B. Tristram, *Natural History of the Bible*.)

The Egyptians also thought that the eclipses of the sun were due to the attacks upon the sun god Ra by the great serpent Apopi, who lived in a celestial river. The sun was supposed to be the ship of Ra which passed across the sky, and when attacked by the serpent it was concealed by the fighting that was going on.

FEAR OF SNAKES

Apparently there have always been two sides to the coin which reflects man's relations with serpents—the positive and the negative. We have examined the former in the section on snake worship, so now let us consider the latter—fear, and the related negative emotions of this hypothetical coin which has, let it be emphasized, a strange penchant for balancing on its edge, no matter how often it is flipped.

Fear of snakes cannot be neatly compartmentalized and isolated from aversion, revulsion, and anger. They overlap, and merge in a combination which describes not only an attitude, but action—the aggressive action on the part of man in his constant war against the snake. Thus it has been since, and in all likelihood was well before, the earliest written records. That observation, of course, brings immediately to mind the biblical archetype of all serpents everywhere—the talking serpent of the Garden of Eden, "more subtile than any beast of the field."

The serpent was given his most familiar comeuppance, of course, in Genesis 3:14: ". . . thou art cursed above all cattle and above

There is no "instinctive" fear of snakes in children or adults; it is a learned response. Properly introduced by parent or teacher, youngsters find snakes fascinating and invariably will touch and handle them despite some previously held aversions.

The young girl holds a Florida kingsnake (*Lampropeltis getulus*). (*Photo: Roy Pinney*) every beast of the field; upon thy belly thou shalt go, and dust shalt thou eat all the days of thy life." Shakespeare, in *King Lear,* had his say in the familiar "How sharper than a serpent's tooth it is to have a thankless child!" and John Milton made reference to the "guile" of the "infernal serpent."

N. P. Christy points out that "in classical Latin, *vipera* means, 'viper! serpent!' a term of reproach," and quotes Matthew 12:34: "Oh generation of vipers how can ye, being evil, speak of good things?"—clarifying the term "generation" as meaning in this instance "brood" or "progeny." Even the scientific nomenclature of snakes, as in *Crotalus horridus,* takes a swipe at the character of the timber rattler. *Horridus,* apart from the obvious, means "frightful, dreadful, awful, uncouth or churlish," sufficient diatribe to put any beast in a bad mood, yet hardly more flattering than *Bothrops atrox,* the taxonomic name for the barba amarilla. He does possess a "pit face," as do all pit vipers, but while the first part of the name does apply, it is doubtful whether he deserves the sum-total opprobrium of "horrid, hideous, atrocious, shocking, revolting, gloomy, sullen, inhuman, fierce, stern and uncompromising"—the dictionary definitions of *atrox.*

What characteristics of the serpent do provoke fear and aversion, hatred and anger? The dread of snakebite and its consequences, based on fact, and related attributes, which are a good deal less than fact, such as reputed aggressiveness. The clinical effects of various venoms on the central nervous system, destruction of blood vessels and tissue, involving hemorrhage, paralysis, convulsions, and other frightful manifestations, must have been even more shocking to observers in a pre-scientific era, for they witnessed the inexplicable and the unknown. It had to be the more terrifying for the victim for the same reason. He could be excused for assuming the fire in his veins was the work of Satan himself. And there was, of course, no antivenin as something upon which to pin hope of relief from agony and escape from death.

Yet the fear of snakes goes beyond the rational dread of their bite and venom. Or the irrational fear of being swallowed alive or crushed to death by a constrictor. Here, myth and legend form a large contributory factor, abetted by drawings of giant sea serpents attacking boats and even ships. Yet there still remains the basic aversion and fright where even a harmless snake is concerned. The sight or the graphic reproduction of a snake's jaws, wide open, fangs bared, quite able to swallow prey of larger dimension than itself, inspires fear and repugnance. The sinuous method of locomotion appears much faster than it actually is. The speed with which a cobra or rattler can strike needs no exaggeration in imagination or description, but here we are not speaking of an actual confrontation, even at a safe distance. Rather, gooseflesh rises from the unconscious recollection of what we have seen in pictures or films, or have read, or have been told. It has often been suggested that this fear is innate, to varying degrees. Inculcation would seem a more likely cause for the automatic reaction of fright. This has been declared the case with children as young as three and a half, still younger children evincing no fear whatever.

Innate or instinctive fear of snakes on the part of animals is another area in which contradictory "evidence" is rife. L. M. Klauber, in his extensive research on the subject pertaining to rattlers, quotes a correspondent as writing: "I have noticed that some horses are alarmed at rattlers and others show no concern at all. . . . I saw a whole pack-string pass a rattler on the very edge of a trail without noticing it. A man on the last horse saw the snake and captured it alive. He then walked by the whole pack-string with the snake in his hand and not one horse showed concern."

Yet a report dated 1765 declared that a group of men on horseback encountered a rattlesnake, and "this so frightened the horses that every one of them screamed or roared." One test with monkeys and apes indicated that they had a natural fear; others with kittens and squirrels indicated the opposite, although the latter, in the wild, warn one another with a motion of the tail.

All in all, if there is any safe generalization on the fear inspired in man by snakes, whether venomous or not, it may be simply this: No "beast of the field," strange and wondrous though his ways may be, can even approach the snake when it comes to the quality of sheer mystery and the unknown. And fear of the unknown, rational or otherwise, is a characteristic of man which itself is mysterious and begs explanation.

MYTHS

Myths, legends, and superstitions about snakes are rife and as wildly exaggerated as the well-known fish story about the one-that-got-away and stories of the he-said-that-she-said-that-he-saw ilk.

Snakes don't milk cows. They can't. They have no sucking mechanism, and even if they did, they couldn't absorb more than a tiny trickle. Nor would the cow put up with so much as the touch of a snake's needle-sharp teeth. Whoever originated this one either had an overstimulated imagination or was tongue-in-cheek and eager for a gullible audience.

The same applies to the anonymous perpetrator of the myth that there exists such a thing as a hoop snake. Tail in mouth, it rolls hither and yon, chasing people and letting them have it with the stinger mounted in its tail. No known snake has ever put together such a vaudeville act of locomotion, nor does any snake have a stinger in its tail.

The eastern milk snake (*Lampropeltis triangulum triangulum*) is often killed because of its superficial resemblance to the copperhead and the ridiculous belief that it milks cows. The young often have bright red blotches that become darker with age. Its length is from 26 to 36 inches, with a record of 52 inches. (*Photo: M. V. Rubio*)

Snakes may appear to stare, but they don't charm or hypnotize their victims. They stare simply because they have no eyelids. The vision of snakes is restricted to comparatively short distances, but within that range is acute. Snakes that are active by day generally have round pupils, while those that move about in the late evening or by night often have vertical pupils.

There is a common belief that the age of a rattlesnake can be determined by the number of rattles encountered on its tail. Not so. A young specimen, which may shed and change its hide as many as three times a year, adds a rattle each time. Older ones may "change clothes" once a year, or not at all, and often rattles fall off and are lost. Thus there is no way of regarding the rattles as beads on an abacus to accurately count a rattler's birthdays.

Size estimates, almost invariably enlarged by fear, extremely brief observation, and the usual inability of the average person to come even close when estimating the length of a room or the width of a stream, are usually far off the mark—on, of course, the exaggerated side. There are, to be sure, the monsters of the tropical forests such as the anaconda and python, but the timber rattlesnake, for example, rarely reaches 5 feet. That is, of course, a lot of snake, but its length gives you an ample safety margin should you encounter one gliding along the ground and he decides, per happy custom, to flee. Also, any living creature of such dimensions is pretty conspicuous and that much more likely to put you on the alert.

Through the centuries, man's imagination has been inspired to glorify or vilify the serpent with weird symbols and powers. The temptation of Eve in the Garden of Eden is countered by the caduceus with two snakes entwining the rod of harmony, representing healing, which was the emblem of the god Mercury. Because of its supposed longevity, it symbolized old age and wisdom. When depicted with its tail in its mouth, it formed the circle, symbol of eternity.

The snake was not killed in South Africa, ancient Greece, and India because of the belief in transmigration—that is, the souls of the dead could appear in snake form. This also gave rise to many supernatural powers attributed to the snake.

What Peter says about Paul is often more revealing about Peter than about Paul. Tales of people being chased by snakes are always suspect. Some snakes such as the black racer or the coachwhip ap-

The amethystine rock python (*Liasis amethystinus*) reaches a length of 20 feet, lives in mangrove trees along the northeastern coast of Australia, and feeds mainly on opossum. (*Photo: Australian News Bureau*)

pear to move very rapidly. When timed, however, it is found that the fastest of snakes, the slender, agile black mamba of Africa, can move only about five miles per hour, and then only in short spurts.

That snakes are slimy and cold to the touch is a common misconception. The aversion is purely psychological. The skin of a snake on land is dry, although some species with smooth, shiny scales appear to be moist. Birds and mammals produce body heat as a by-product of metabolic activity. The metabolic rate of snakes does not produce enough internal heat, and the snake's body temperature is therefore closely related to the temperature of its environment. On a cold day, an exposed snake will feel cold to the touch. A snake basking in the sun for any length of time will feel warm.

Snakes do not swallow their young in times of danger to protect them. Some snakes eat other snakes as part of their diet. Some snakes lay eggs, others are live-bearing, and the finding of baby snakes inside the body of the mother may have led to this most prevalent of snake myths.

Another persistent superstition out West where the cowboys roam is that rattlesnakes will not cross over a horsehair or cowhair rope. In the pioneer days, when sleeping on the ground was often necessary, to protect himself a man placed a lariat around his blanket to keep the rattlesnakes away. Surrounding oneself with a symbolic circle as a charm and protection against danger is a superstition that goes back in antiquity. Rattlesnakes or other snakes would not hesitate to crawl over a rope on the ground.

Many other fables about snakes have become folklore: that the killing of a snake will be avenged by its mate; that whiskey is a cure for snakebite; that "snake oil" is a cure for rheumatism and other ailments; the glass snake that shatters into fragments when struck; and scores of other tales.

DON'T TREAD ON ME!

The rattlesnake symbol was widely used during the Revolution. It appeared on flags, drums, Continental currency, etc., in different parts of the country, usually bearing the legend that virtually became a battle cry: "Don't tread on me!"

The first Navy jack with a rattlesnake spread across the thirteen stripes is typical of the temperament of the times in which it was created. It appears again and again in the early colonial flags. The rattlesnake motif was used by the South Carolina navy and by the minutemen of Culpeper County, Virginia. It was flown as a "jack" from the bow of the *Alfred* when that vessel was the flagship of Commodore Esek Hopkins, whose fleet made a successful raid on New Providence in the Bahamas in 1776. The rattlesnake design was gradually abandoned as a more permanent type of flag came into use.

The Gadsden flag was another famous rattlesnake flag of Revolutionary days. On its yellow field it had a coiled rattler with the words "Don't Tread on Me!" Christopher Gadsden, a South Carolina delegate to the Second Continental Congress, presented this flag to the Congress in 1776 to have it become the flag for the commander in chief of the American Navy during the Revolutionary War but was unsuccessful in having it so recognized.

The unknown author of a remarkable letter published in Bradford's *Journal* dated December 27, 1775, wrote the following about the rattlesnake as a national emblem. It displays a surprising familiarity with the natural history of the reptile in the accuracy of his analogies.

Messrs. Printers:

I have observed on one of the drums belonging to the marines, now raising, there was painted a rattlesnake with this modest motto under it: "Don't tread on me!" As I know it is the custom to have some device on the arms of every country, I sat down to guess what might have been intended by this uncommon device. I took care, however, to consult on this occasion a person acquainted with heraldry, from whom I learned that it is a rule among the learned that the worthy properties of an animal in a crest shall be considered, and that the base ones cannot have been intended. He likewise informed me that the ancients regarded the serpent as an emblem of wisdom, and in a certain attitude, of endless duration, both of which circumstance may have been in view. Having gained this intelligence, and recollecting that countries are sometimes represented by animals peculiar to them, it occurred to me that the rattlesnake is found in no other quarter of the globe than America, and it may therefore have been chosen on that account to represent

her. But then, the worthy properties of the snake would be hard
to point out. This rather raised than suppressed my curiosity,
and having frequently seen the rattlesnake, I ran over in my
mind every property for which she was distinguished, not only
from other animals but from those of the same class, endeavor-
ing to fix some meaning to each not wholly inconsistent with
common sense. I recollected that her eye exceeded in brilliance
that of any other animal and that she has no eyelids. She may
therefore be esteemed an emblem of vigilance. She never begins
an attack, nor when once engaged, ever surrenders. She is therefore an emblem of magnanimity and true courage. As if anxious
to prevent all pretensions of quarreling with the weapons with
which nature favored her, she conceals them in the roof of her
mouth, so that to those who are unacquainted with her, she appears to be defenceless; and even when those weapons are
shown and extended for defence, they appear weak and con-
temptible; but their wounds, however small, are decisive and
fatal. Conscious of this she never wounds until she has gen-
erously given notice even to her enemy, and cautioned her
against the danger of treading on her. Was I wrong, sirs, in
thinking this is a strong picture of the temper and conduct of
America?

The poison of her teeth is the necessary means of digesting
her food, and at the same time is the certain destruction of her
enemies. This may be understood to intimate that those things
which are destructive to our enemies may be to us not only
harmless but absolutely necessary to our existence. I confess I
was totally at a loss what to make of the rattles until I went
back and counted them, and found them just 13—exactly the
number of colonies united in America, and I recollected too,
that this was the only part of the snake that increased in numbers. . . . 'Tis curious and amazing to observe how distinct
and independent of each other the rattles of this animal are, and
yet how firmly they are united together so as to be never separated except by breaking them to pieces. One of these rattles,
singly, is incapable of producing sound; but the ringing of thirteen together is sufficient to alarm the boldest men living. The
rattlesnake is solitary and associates with her kind only when it
is necessary for her preservation. In winter the warmth of a

number together will preserve their lives, whilst singly they would probably perish. The power of fascination attributed to her by a generous construction may be understood to mean that those who consider the liberty and blessings which America affords, and once come over to her, never afterwards leave her, but spend their lives with her. She strongly resembles America in this; that she is beautiful in youth and her beauty increases with age; her tongue also is blue, and forked as lightning, and her abode is among impenetrable rocks.

LEGALITIES

Many local communities throughout the country have ordinances similar to the provisos in New York City's Health Code, which prohibits the possession of dangerous animals on premises within the city limits. Venomous snakes are dangerous, to the experienced as well as the inexperienced, the amateur and the professional alike. While there are relatively few deaths due to snakebite, they nevertheless do occur each year. Statistics on nonfatal snakebite cases do not reflect the pain, fear, shock, and general ordeal, or the medical expenses involved. Why, then, take chances? If self-confidence is such that the feeling is: "I won't be bitten or harmed in any way because I know what I'm doing," what about the leading herpetologists who have succumbed to snakebite? It can happen to anybody.

Abiding by a few basic precautions can spell the difference between safety and tragedy. Extreme caution in handling dangerous snakes is, obviously, a prime requisite. Snakes which pose a threat should be kept in sturdily built cages, with no avenue of escape, and the cages should be kept locked—behind locked doors when possible.

The New York law states, in effect, that no resident may keep a venomous or dangerous snake unless he applies for and receives a permit from the Commissioner of Health. Likewise, dealers and those engaged in the production of antivenin must obtain a permit. Zoological parks, licensed laboratories and aquariums, scientific and educational institutions, plus a circus or sideshow which has ample protectve devices to prevent escape, can purchase or receive venomous snakes.

Inasmuch as the law's wording in reference to the prohibited rep-

Dr. Vivian FitzSimons, author of *Snakes of Southern Africa*, is shown with a young African python (*Python sebae*), by far the largest snake found in Africa, with adults averaging 12 to 15 feet. Though quite nonvenomous, the needle-sharp, recurved teeth can inflict a nasty wound which, owing to the foulness of the snake's mouth, often leads to blood poisoning if not properly treated immediately.

When disturbed or alarmed, according to Dr. FitzSimons, pythons are not unduly prone to attack, but usually attempt to escape as quickly as possible; on the other hand, it must always be realized that a specimen of 10 feet or more can be dangerous if cornered and is quite capable of constricting an aggressor. In such an emergency, uncoiling the snake is best effected from the tail end, as the power of the muscles is thus more easily overcome, and secondly, an approach to the head end is much more difficult and dangerous owing to the risk of receiving a savage bite. In captivity they are easily tamed and make intelligent and interesting pets, although they usually appear lethargic in confinement. (*Photo: SA-TOUR*) tiles was broadly stated, omitting any specific references to which snakes were deemed "venomous and dangerous," the following list was compiled by Dr. Herndon G. Dowling for the New York Herpetological Society:

(1) All front-fanged venomous snakes.
(2) The following South African rear-fanged snakes:
    a. Striped skaapsteker (*Psammophylax tritaeniatus*)
    b. Rhombic, or spotted, skaapsteker (*Psammophylax rhombeatus*)
    c. Boomslang (*Dispholidus typus*)
    d. Bird snake (*Thelotornis kirtlandii*)
    e. Natal blacksnake (*Macrelaps microlepidotus*)
(3) Any constricting snake over 8 feet in length.

Boas and pythons are capable of severe bites. The length "limitation" of 8 feet does not imply that a 7-foot boa or python is to be disregarded as completely harmless. But the smaller ones are considerably less formidable, and a line does have to be drawn somewhere.

In summation, there are enough easily obtainable harmless species of snakes to serve for study purposes and/or pets. Thus it hardly seems necessary to occupy oneself with the dangerous forms, and risk not only personal but public safety as well.

Opportunities in Herpetology

COLLECTING BOOKS

One of the residual pleasures of any hobby is to read and collect the literature on the subject. An appealing by-product about books on reptiles is that they can be a worthwhile financial investment which may become a passionate pursuit in itself.

Books and pamphlets about snakes are available from various trade publishers, either directly or through bookstores, governmental agencies, museums, and universities, from the authors directly, and from book dealers, who often advertise in the herpetological publications. Many so-called rare books are still available, often at a bargain price that has remained the same over the years since they were published, by simply ordering from the publisher. Friends with similar interests may have books to swap. Surplus books are sometimes available from libraries that simply don't have the room to store them. Individuals and estates occasionally offer a complete library to the highest bidder at advertised auctions.

Rare books are an interesting investment. Their values have been climbing an estimated 10 to 20 per cent a year and, in some cases, even more. Books as an investment, however, can't be bought on hunches. As with stocks, you have to know what you're buying and why.

First editions, if in mint condition, are considered more valuable than later printings. If they are signed by the author, they are worth more. A first edition is more valuable than a later one for several reasons. A first represents the initial appearance of an author's creative effort and thus enjoys a distinction that can never be attached to subsequent printings. It also has a scarcity value because of the limited number of books that were printed and remain available. A third element is really a combination of the previous two: the law of supply and demand governs the rare-book field, and the fewer copies available of a favored author's works, the dearer the books.

This raises the question of what to collect. The decision has to be yours. A rare volume that makes one bookworm shrug may be a prize to another. Some collectors set goals—all the first of one author, say, or all the significant books on a particular subject or of a geographic area. The basic precept of collecting is to buy what interests you and gives you pleasure.

HERPETOLOGY AS A PROFESSION

Herpetology is the branch of zoology dealing with reptiles and amphibians. The small boy with a pet turtle, the keeper who feeds reptiles in a zoo, or the operator of a roadside snake show may consider himself a herpetologist, but for our purposes he is best defined as one who, by virtue of his applied knowledge, contributes to this science. There are numerous approaches, such as studying the embryology of frogs, the behavior of lizards, the taxonomy of salamanders, or the geographic distribution of snakes. If the student concentrates on amphibians primarily to gain knowledge of embryology, he may well call himself an embryologist. However, if he seeks a clearer knowledge of amphibians via a study of their embryology, he probably thinks of himself as a herpetologist.

The American Society of Herpetologists at the National Museum of Natural History, Washington, D.C., has published a comprehensive survey of the job structure in the field which includes educational requirements and salaries for positions in various categories, along the following lines:

Museums: At the top of the ladder, we have the curator. There are perhaps 15–20 full-time positions in this category. Openings are rare. Salaries for these coveted positions range from $10,000 to $30,000. Duties include research, caring for collections, preparing exhibits, and administrative chores. Museums maintaining research collections usually provide the curator with one or more assistants at the technician level.

Small public museums, combined library-museums, and so-called nature centers have small staffs. Employees other than the director rarely are paid more than $10,000 per annum.

Zoos: Several of the major zoos employ a herpetologist as curator. He is responsible for maintaining exhibits and disseminating knowledge via the media. Salary is rarely over $20,000. He may have two or three animal keepers to aid him, selected because of demonstrated ability in handling and caring for live reptiles and amphibians. Careers as keepers may be long on security, but short in advancement.

Teaching: Most herpetologists today are hired as teachers in colleges and universities. Research is encouraged, via funding for field trips and expeditions. Usually an advanced degree in biology is required. Pay ranges from $10,000 to $30,000 and, rarely, up to $35,000 in the case of some of the endowed chairs. A wider, if less prestigious field is that of teaching biology in high schools and junior colleges.

Research: Occasionally there are openings for the full-time herpetologist in the U. S. Fish and Wildlife Service, state conservation departments, and biological or natural history surveys. Usually these are under Civil Service. Salaries are competitive with nongovernment rates. Positions in industry usually require research which relates to the services and goals of the enterprise concerned. A relatively new job slot for the herpetologist is that of environmental consultant for engineering firms and government environmental protection agencies. Usually, graduate degrees are required; the consultant must be able to prepare environmental analyses, write well, and have a sound background in the literature of the field. Starting salaries: $10,000 to $15,000.

Reptile and Amphibian Sales: Commercial enterprises include pet shops, research and venom-collecting labs, public displays, and mail-order houses which supply animals to zoos, research laboratories, and amateur collectors. Requirements here are business acumen, a flair for publicity, and some knowledge of the care and handling of animals. Increasingly stringent government regulations, however, are making it ever more difficult to sell and ship live reptiles. Only a few of such ventures survive. Venom collection for medical and research purposes is carried out by a number of commercial firms, but the demand is limited and competition severe.

Getting into the Field: As is evidenced by the foregoing, few herpetologists are employed full-time in their specialty. Most hold down other jobs which permit part-time studies. The aspirant is urged to follow their example, and bear in mind the importance of formal education—specifically, an advanced degree in biology or zoology, which is a must for college teaching or research. The student must *not* ignore the importance of peripheral studies such as mathematics, chemistry, physics, and foreign languages.

Several major universities in the United States offer graduate work in biology with herpetology as a specialty. Teaching assistant and research assistant jobs are often available to the graduate student, paying $1,200 to $3,000 or more on a part-time basis. Biggest hurdles are the time required (four to six years beyond a bachelor's degree), the basic scholastic requirements, the successful completion of a research project, plus the preparation and defense of a dissertation.

The professional herpetologist is expected to be an expert on the subject of snakebite, is often asked to address local schools, clubs, and civic organizations. Also he must find time to devote to administrative chores, public relations, editorial tasks, and so on.

A Few Tips: Recommended study sources include: *Introduction to Herpetology,* by K. R. Porter (W. B. Saunders Co., 1972), and *The Natural History of North American Amphibians and Reptiles,* by J. A. Oliver (D. Van Nostrand Co., 1955). Aids for identification: *A Field Guide to Reptiles and Amphibians of the United States and Canada East of the 100th Meridian,* by R. Conant (Houghton Mifflin Co., 1975). These books list additional references dealing with particular reptile and amphibian groups.

It is advisable to make the acquaintance of active herpetologists, often found on the staff of a local college and museums and zoos of larger cities. Usually they are helpful and patient with the beginner. The young amateur should become acquainted with the herpetological societies and publications listed on following pages. Special student membership rates are usually available.

HERPETOLOGICAL SOCIETIES

American Society of Ichthyologists and Herpetologists
U. S. National Museum
Washington, D.C. 20560

British Herpetological Society
Zoological Society, Regents Park
London, N.W.1, England

Chicago Herpetological Society
2001 North Clark Street
Chicago, Ill. 60614

Herpetologists' League
1041 New Hampshire Street
Lawrence, Kans. 66044

Kansas Herpetological Society
Topeka Zoological Park
Topeka, Kans. 66606

New York Herpetological Society
P. O. Box 3945, Grand Central Station
New York, N.Y. 10017

Society for the Study of Amphibians and Reptiles
Department of Zoology
Ohio University, Athens, Ohio 45701

HERPETOLOGICAL PUBLICATIONS

British Journal of Herpetology
Zoological Society of London
Regents Park, London, N.W.1, England

Bulletin
Chicago Herpetological Society
2001 North Clark Street
Chicago, Ill. 60614

Copeia
American Society of Herpetologists
34th Street and Girard Avenue
Philadelphia, Pa.

Journal of Herpetology
University of Kansas
Lawrence, Kans. 66044

Herp
New York Herpetological Society
P. O. Box 3945, Grand Central Station
New York, N.Y. 10017

Herpetological
1041 New Hampshire Street
Lawrence, Kans. 66044

Appendix

CLASSIFICATION OF SNAKES

In 1758, Carolus Linnaeus published his *Systema Naturae,* in which he introduced binomial (genus and species) names for animals and the concepts of higher classification, such as class and phylum. Although some may find scientific names difficult, they are necessary even for the serious amateur naturalist. We are often faced with animals that have several common names. This can be confusing to the point that people in one region may not recognize the names used in another. For example, the yellow rat snake (*Elaphe obsoleta quadrivittata*) is also known as the striped house snake, striped rat snake, Everglades rat snake, and chicken snake. *Vipera russelii* is commonly known as Russell's viper, daboia, and tic polonga. "Fer-de-lance" is erroneously applied to several Central and South American vipers. The true fer-de-lance occurs only on Martinique.

Because there is an International Commission which regulates the use of scientific names around the world, the scientific names of snakes or any other animals will be recognized in any country regardless of language, whereas common names obviously will not.

In addition to standardizing the nomenclature for animals, the modified Linnaean system which we use today, a system of hierarchical classification, allows us to pigeonhole information pertinent to the animal. Each taxonomic rank is contained within higher ranks, and being a member of a certain group implies much additional information from the higher taxa of which that group is a part. Thus, the name *Crotalus atrox* identifies a common rattlesnake, but also indirectly tells us that it is a pit viper, because it is in the subfamily

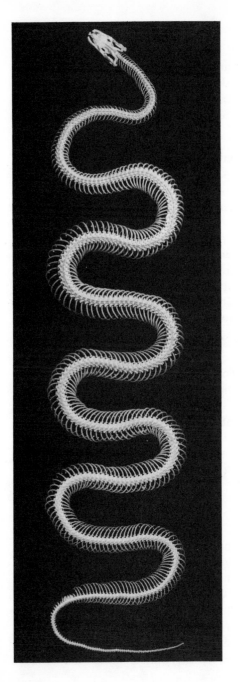

The classification of snakes
has been heavily dependent
on the decisions (often
unexplained) of individual
taxonomists and the weight
that they apply to the
variations of different
structures. The vertebral
structure has often been the
mainstay for understanding
relationships. (*Illustration:
British Museum*)

Crotalinae; a venomous viper, because it is in the family Viperidae; and an advanced snake with many skeletal modifications, because it is in the superfamily Colubroidea.

There are some 417 genera and 2,340 species of snakes in the world that may be classified in eleven families, according to H. G. Dowling:

(1) Boidae	Pythons and boas	59	species
(2) Aniliidae	Pipe snakes	9	species
(3) Tropidophiidae	Wood snakes	20	species
(4) Bolyeriidae	Mauritius snakes	2	species
(5) Uropeltidae	Shield-tailed snakes	44	species
(6) Leptotyphlopidae	Slender blind snakes	96	species
(7) Anomalepididae	Primitive blind snakes	18	species
(8) Typhlopoidae	Blind snakes	150	species
(9) Colubridae	Typical snakes	1,518	species
(10) Elapidae	Cobras and allies	244	species
(11) Viperidae	Vipers	180	species

Of the total number of snakes recognized, there are 424 venomous forms.

Classifications attempt to show phylogeny, or the evolutionary history of lineages and their relationships, as well as superficial similarity. Ideally, a classification should show cladogenesis, or sister groups descended from a common ancestor, but even the best herpetologists will admit that current knowledge of snake relationships and the poor fossil record are such that we are happy to know that two snakes are related at all, let alone closely related.

SCIENTIFIC LANGUAGE

The basic language of scientific names in zoology is Latin, and names from other languages are Latinized or treated as such. The English equivalents of Latin names, formidable as they sometimes look to the unfamiliar eye, are not too difficult to understand. Armed with a few stems such as *ophis* (snake), *pellis* (skin), *ops* (eye), *scutum* (scale), *stomus* (mouth), *urus* (tail), *notus* (back), and *venter* (belly), one is well launched in understanding the formation of the names of snakes of the United States and Canada.

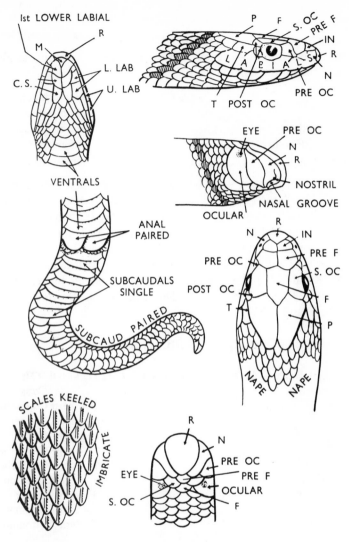

Abbreviated nomenclature of a snake's scales:

R = rostral; In = internasals; N = Nasal; Pre F = prefrontals; **Pre Oc** = preocular; F = frontal; P = parietal; Post Oc = postocular; T = temporal; M = mental; C.S. = chin shields; L. lab = lower labials; U. lab = upper labials.

The upper and lower labials border the lips.

The ventrals are the broad plates under the belly.

The anals cover the anal opening.

The subcaudals are under the tail.

Scale rows are counted obliquely as indicated by black scales in the two figures at the top right. (*Illustration: J. R. Kinghorn*)

Several classical color names have been taken over in English. Some of the more common are:

albus: white	*cinereus:* ashy	*niger:* black
ater: black	*cupreus:* coppery	*purpureus:* purple
aureus: golden	*flavus:* light yellow	*roseus:* rosy
brunneus: deep brown	*leucus:* white	*ruber:* red
caeruleus: blue	*luteus:* yellow	*viridis:* green

To the color names should be added a few common pattern names such as: *annulatus* (ringed), *cinctus* (girdled), *fasciatus* (banded), *lineatus* (lined), *maculatus* (spotted), *punctatus* (dotted).

Snakes have scales (*lepis, pholis*) and teeth (*odonta*). Some species are named in honor of an individual: *agassizi* (L. Agassiz), *blanchardi* (F. N. Blanchard), *kirtlandi* (J. P. Kirtland), *klauberi* (L. M. Klauber), etc. Some describers of American snakes include R. Conant, F. D. Cope, R. L. Ditmars, H. G. Dowling, M. B. Mittleman, and J. Van Denburgh.

NORTH AMERICAN SNAKES

AGKISTRODON — COPPERHEADS AND COTTONMOUTHS

A. contortrix	Copperhead
A. c. contortrix	Southern Copperhead
A. c. laticinctus	Broad-banded Copperhead
A. c. mokeson	Northern Copperhead
A. c. phaeogaster	Osage Copperhead
A. c. pictigaster	Trans-Pecos Copperhead
A. piscivorus	Cottonmouth
A. p. conanti	Florida Cottonmouth
A. p. leucostoma	Southern Cottonmouth
A. p. piscivorus	Eastern Cottonmouth

ARIZONA — GLOSSY SNAKES

A. elegans	Glossy Snake
A. e. arenicola	Texas Glossy Snake
A. e. candida	Mohave Glossy Snake
A. e. eburnata	Desert Glossy Snake
A. e. elegans	Kansas Glossy Snake
A. e. noctivaga	Arizona Glossy Snake
A. e. occidentalis	California Glossy Snake
A. e. philipi	Painted Desert Glossy Snake

CARPHOPHIS — WORM SNAKES
C. amoenus   Worm Snake
   C. a. amoenus   Eastern Worm Snake
   C. a. helenae   Midwest Worm Snake
   C. a. vermis   Western Worm Snake

CEMOPHORA — SCARLET SNAKES
C. coccinea   Scarlet Snake
   C. c. coccinea   Florida Scarlet Snake
   C. c. copei   Northern Scarlet Snake
   C. c. lineri   Texas Scarlet Snake

CHARINA — RUBBER BOAS
C. bottae   Rubber Boa

CHILOMENISCUS — SAND SNAKES
C. cinctus   Banded Sand Snake

CHIONACTIS — SHOVELNOSE SNAKES
C. occipitalis   Western Shovelnose Snake
   C. o. annulata   Colorado Desert Shovelnose Snake
   C. o. klauberi   Tucson Shovelnose Snake
   C. o. occipitalis   Mojave Shovelnose Snake
   C. o. talpina   Nevada Shovelnose Snake
C. palarostris   Sonoran Shovelnose Snake
   C. p. organica   Organ Pipe Shovelnose Snake
C. saxatilis   Mountain Shovelnose Snake

CLONOPHIS — KIRTLAND'S SNAKES
C. kirtlandi   Kirtland's Snake

COLUBER — RACERS
C. constrictor   Racer
   C. c. anthicus   Buttermilk Racer
   C. c. constrictor   Northern Black Racer
   C. c. etheridgei   Tan Racer
   C. c. flaviventris   Eastern Yellowbelly Racer
   C. c. helvigularis   Brownchin Racer
   C. c. latrunculus   Blackmask Racer
   C. c. mormon   Western Yellowbelly Racer
   C. c. oaxaca   Mexican Racer
   C. c. paludicola   Everglades Racer
   C. c. priapus   Southern Black Racer

CONIOPHANES — BLACK-STRIPED SNAKES
C. imperialis — Black-striped Snake
    C. i. imperialis — Black-striped Snake

CONTIA — SHARPTAIL SNAKES
C. tenuis — Sharptail Snake

CROTALUS — RATTLESNAKES
C. adamanteus — Eastern Diamondback Rattlesnake
C. atrox — Western Diamondback Rattlesnake
C. cerastes — Sidewinder
    C. c. cerastes — Mojave Desert Sidewinder
    C. c. cercobombus — Sonoran Sidewinder
    C. c. laterorepens — Colorado Desert Sidewinder
C. horridus — Timber Rattlesnake
C. lepidus — Rock Rattlesnake
    C. l. klauberi — Banded Rock Rattlesnake
    C. l. lepidus — Mottled Rock Rattlesnake
C. mitchelli — Speckled Rattlesnake
    C. m. pyrrhus — Southwestern Speckled Rattlesnake
    C. m. stephensi — Panamint Rattlesnake
C. molossus — Blacktail Rattlesnake
    C. m. molossus — Blacktail Rattlesnake
C. pricei — Twin-spotted Rattlesnake
    C. p. pricei — Twin-spotted Rattlesnake
C. ruber — Red Diamond Rattlesnake
    C. r. ruber — Red Diamond Rattlesnake
C. scutulatus — Mojave Rattlesnake
    C. s. scutulatus — Mojave Rattlesnake
C. tigris — Tiger Rattlesnake
C. viridis — Western Rattlesnake
    C. v. abyssus — Grand Canyon Rattlesnake
    C. v. cerberus — Arizona Black Rattlesnake
    C. v. concolor — Midget Faded Rattlesnake
    C. v. helleri — Southern Pacific Rattlesnake
    C. v. lutosus — Great Basin Rattlesnake
    C. v. nuntius — Hopi Rattlesnake
    C. v. oreganus — Northern Pacific Rattlesnake
    C. v. viridis — Prairie Rattlesnake
C. willardi — Ridgenose Rattlesnake
    C. w. obscurus — New Mexico Ridgenose Rattlesnake
    C. w. willardi — Arizona Ridgenose Rattlesnake

DIADOPHIS — RINGNECK SNAKES

D. punctatus	Ringneck Snake
D. p. acricus	Key Ringneck Snake
D. p. amabilis	Pacific Ringneck Snake
D. p. arnyi	Prairie Ringneck Snake
D. p. edwardsi	Northern Ringneck Snake
D. p. modestus	San Bernardino Ringneck Snake
D. p. occidentalis	Northwestern Ringneck Snake
D. p. pulchellus	Coralbelly Ringneck Snake
D. p. punctatus	Southern Ringneck Snake
D. p. regalis	Regal Ringneck Snake
D. p. similis	San Diego Ringneck Snake
D. p. stictogenys	Mississippi Ringneck Snake
D. p. vandenburghi	Monterey Ringneck Snake

DRYMARCHON — INDIGO SNAKES

D. corais	Indigo Snake
D. c. couperi	Eastern Indigo Snake
D. c. erebennus	Texas Indigo Snake

DRYMOBIUS — SPECKLED RACERS

D. margaritiferus	Speckled Racer
D. m. margaritiferus	Speckled Racer

ELAPHE — RAT SNAKES

E. guttata	Corn Snake
E. g. emoryi	Great Plains Rat Snake
E. g. guttata	Corn Snake
E. obsoleta	Rat Snake
E. o. bairdi	Baird's Rat Snake
E. o. lindheimeri	Texas Rat Snake
E. o. obsoleta	Black Rat Snake
E. o. quadrivittata	Yellow Rat Snake
E. o. rossalleni	Everglades Rat Snake
E. o. spiloides	Gray Rat Snake
E. o. williamii	Blotched Rat Snake
E. subocularis	Trans-Pecos Rat Snake
E. triaspis	Green Rat Snake
E. t. intermedia	Green Rat Snake
E. vulpina	Fox Snake
E. v. gloydi	Eastern Fox Snake
E. v. vulpina	Western Fox Snake

FARANCIA — MUD AND RAINBOW SNAKES
F. abacura   Mud Snake
   F. a. abacura   Eastern Mud Snake
   F. a. reinwardti   Western Mud Snake
F. erytrogramma   Rainbow Snake
   F. e. erytrogramma   Rainbow Snake
   F. e. seminola   South Florida Rainbow Snake

FICIMIA — MEXICAN HOOKNOSE SNAKES
F. streckeri   Mexican Hooknose Snake

GYALOPION — PLATEAU HOOKNOSE SNAKES
G. canum   Western Hooknose Snake
G. quadrangularis   Desert Hooknose Snake

HETERODON — HOGNOSE SNAKES
H. nasicus   Western Hognose Snake
   H. n. gloydi   Dusty Hognose Snake
   H. n. kennerlyi   Mexican Hognose Snake
   H. n. nasicus   Plains Hognose Snake
H. platyrhinos   Eastern Hognose Snake
H. simus   Southern Hognose Snake

HYPSIGLENA — NIGHT SNAKES
H. torquata   Night Snake
   H. t. deserticola   Desert Night Snake
   H. t. jani   Texas Night Snake
   H. t. klauberi   San Diego Night Snake
   H. t. loreala   Mesa Verde Night Snake
   H. t. nuchalata   California Night Snake
   H. t. ochrorhyncha   Spotted Night Snake

LAMPROPELTIS — KINGSNAKES AND MILK SNAKES
L. calligaster   Prairie Kingsnake
   L. c. calligaster   Prairie Kingsnake
   L. c. rhombomaculata   Mole Kingsnake
L. getulus   Common Kingsnake
   L. g. californiae   California Kingsnake
   L. g. floridana   Florida Kingsnake
   L. g. getulus   Eastern Kingsnake
   L. g. holbrooki   Speckled Kingsnake
   L. g. niger   Black Kingsnake
   L. g. nigritus   Mexican Kingsnake
   L. g. splendida   Desert Kingsnake

L. mexicana	Gray-banded Kingsnake
L. m. alterna	Gray-banded Kingsnake
L. pyromelana	Sonoran Mountain Kingsnake
L. p. infralabialis	Utah Mountain Kingsnake
L. p. pyromelana	Arizona Mountain Kingsnake
L. p. woodini	Huachuca Mountain Kingsnake
L. triangulum	Milk Snake
L. t. amaura	Louisiana Milk Snake
L. t. annulata	Mexican Milk Snake
L. t. celaenops	Mexico Milk Snake
L. t. elapsoides	Scarlet Kingsnake
L. t. gentilis	Central Plains Milk Snake
L. t. multistrata	Pale Milk Snake
L. t. syspila	Red Milk Snake
L. t. taylori	Utah Milk Snake
L. t. triangulum	Eastern Milk Snake
L. zonata	California Mountain Kingsnake
L. z. multicincta	Sierra Mountain Kingsnake
L. z. multifasciata	Coast Mountain Kingsnake
L. z. parvirubra	San Bernardino Mountain Kingsnake
L. z. pulchra	San Diego Mountain Kingsnake
L. z. zonata	Saint Helena Mountain Kingsnake

LEPTODEIRA — CAT-EYED SNAKES
L. septentrionalis	Cat-eyed Snake
L. s. septentrionalis	Northern Cat-eyed Snake

LEPTOTYPHLOPS — BLIND SNAKES
L. dulcis	Texas Blind Snake
L. d. dissectus	New Mexico Blind Snake
L. d. dulcis	Plains Blind Snake
L. humilis	Western Blind Snake
L. h. cahuilae	Desert Blind Snake
L. h. humilis	Southwestern Blind Snake
L. h. segregus	Trans-Pecos Blind Snake
L. h. utahensis	Utah Blind Snake

LICHANURA — ROSY BOAS
L. trivirgata	Rosy Boa
L. t. gracia	Desert Rosy Boa
L. t. roseofusca	Coastal Rosy Boa
L. t. trivirgata	Mexican Rosy Boa

MASTICOPHIS — WHIPSNAKES AND COACHWHIPS

M. bilineatus	Sonoran Whipsnake
M. b. bilineatus	Sonoran Whipsnake
M. b. lineolatus	Ajo Mountain Whipsnake
M. flagellum	Coachwhip
M. f. cingulum	Sonoran Coachwhip
M. f. flagellum	Eastern Coachwhip
M. f. fuliginosus	Baja California Coachwhip
M. f. lineatus	Lined Coachwhip
M. f. piceus	Red Coachwhip
M. f. ruddocki	San Joaquin Coachwhip
M. f. testaceus	Western Coachwhip
M. lateralis	Striped Racer
M. l. euryxanthus	Alameda Striped Racer
M. l. lateralis	California Striped Racer
M. taeniatus	Striped Whipsnake
M. t. ornatus	Central Texas Whipsnake
M. t. ruthveni	Ruthven's Whipsnake
M. t. schotti	Schott's Whipsnake
M. t. taeniatus	Desert Striped Whipsnake

MICRUROIDES — WESTERN CORAL SNAKES

M. euryxanthus	Arizona Coral Snake
M. e. euryxanthus	Arizona Coral Snake

MICRURUS — EASTERN CORAL SNAKES

M. fulvius	Eastern Coral Snake
M. f. fulvius	Eastern Coral Snake
M. f. tenere	Texas Coral Snake

NERODIA — WATER SNAKES AND SALT MARSH SNAKES

N. cyclopion	Green Water Snake
N. c. cyclopion	Green Water Snake
N. c. floridana	Florida Green Water Snake
N. erythrogaster	Plainbelly Water Snake
N. e. erythrogaster	Redbelly Water Snake
N. e. flavigaster	Yellowbelly Water Snake
N. e. neglecta	Copperbelly Water Snake
N. e. transversa	Blotched Water Snake
N. fasciata	Southern Water Snake
N. f. clarki	Gulf Salt Marsh Snake
N. f. compressicauda	Mangrove Salt Marsh Snake
N. f. confluens	Broad-banded Water Snake
N. f. fasciata	Banded Water Snake

N. f. pictiventris   Florida Water Snake
N. f. taeniata   Atlantic Salt Marsh Snake
N. harteri   Harter's Water Snake
  N. h. harteri   Brazos Water Snake
  N. h. paucimaculata   Concho Water Snake
N. rhombifera   Diamondback Water Snake
  N. r. rhombifera   Diamondback Water Snake
N. sipedon   Northern Water Snake
  N. s. insularum   Lake Erie Water Snake
  N. s. pleuralis   Midland Water Snake
  N. s. sipedon   Northern Water Snake
  N. s. williamengelsi   Carolina Salt Marsh Snake
N. taxispilota   Brown Water Snake

OPHEODRYS — GREEN SNAKES
O. aestivus   Rough Green Snake
O. vernalis   Smooth Green Snake
  O. v. blanchardi   Western Smooth Green Snake
  O. v. vernalis   Eastern Smooth Green Snake

OXYBELIS — VINE SNAKES
O. aeneus   Mexican Vine Snake

PHYLLORHYNCHUS — LEAFNOSE SNAKES
P. browni   Saddled Leafnose Snake
  P. b. browni   Pima Leafnose Snake
  P. b. lucidus   Maricopa Leafnose Snake
P. decurtatus   Spotted Leafnose Snake
  P. d. nubilis   Clouded Leafnose Snake
  P. d. perkinsi   Western Leafnose Snake

PITUOPHIS — BULLSNAKES, PINE SNAKES AND GOPHER SNAKES
P. melanoleucus   Pine Snake (Eastern U.S. subspecies)
  P. m. lodingi   Black Pine Snake
  P. m. melanoleucus   Northern Pine Snake
  P. m. mugitus   Florida Pine Snake
  P. m. ruthveni   Louisiana Pine Snake
P. melanoleucus   Gopher Snake (Western U.S. subspecies)
  P. m. affinis   Sonoran Gopher Snake
  P. m. annectans   San Diego Gopher Snake
  P. m. catenifer   Pacific Gopher Snake

P. m. deserticola   Great Basin Gopher Snake
P. m. pumilis   Santa Cruz Gopher Snake
P. m. sayi   Bullsnake

REGINA — CRAYFISH SNAKES
R. alleni   Striped Crayfish Snake
R. grahami   Graham's Crayfish Snake
R. rigida   Glossy Crayfish Snake
    R. r. deltae   Delta Crayfish Snake
    R. r. rigida   Glossy Crayfish Snake
    R. r. sinicola   Gulf Crayfish Snake
R. septemvittata   Queen Snake

RHADINAEA — PINE WOODS SNAKES
R. flavilata   Pine Woods Snake

RHINOCHEILUS — LONGNOSE SNAKES
R. lecontei   Longnose Snake
    R. l. lecontei   Western Longnose Snake
    R. l. tessellatus   Texas Longnose Snake

SALVADORA — PATCHNOSE SNAKES
S. deserticola   Big Bend Patchnose Snake
S. grahamiae   Mountain Patchnose Snake
    S. g. grahamiae   Mountain Patchnose Snake
    S. g. lineata   Texas Patchnose Snake
S. hexalepis   Western Patchnose Snake
    S. h. hexalepis   Desert Patchnose Snake
    S. h. mojavensis   Mojave Patchnose Snake
    S. h. virgultea   Coast Patchnose Snake

SEMINATRIX — SWAMP SNAKES
S. pygaea   Black Swamp Snake
    S. p. cyclas   South Florida Swamp Snake
    S. p. paludis   Carolina Swamp Snake
    S. p. pygaea   North Florida Swamp Snake

SISTRURUS — PIGMY RATTLESNAKES AND MASSASAUGAS
S. catenatus   Massasauga
    S. c. catenatus   Eastern Massasauga
    S. c. edwardsi   Desert Massasauga
    S. c. tergeminus   Western Massasauga
S. miliarius   Pigmy Rattlesnake
    S. m. barbouri   Dusky Pigmy Rattlesnake
    S. m. miliarius   Carolina Pigmy Rattlesnake
    S. m. streckeri   Western Pigmy Rattlesnake

SONORA — GROUND SNAKES

S. episcopa	Ground Snake
S. e. episcopa	Great Plains Ground Snake
S. e. taylori	South Texas Ground Snake
S. semiannulata	Western Ground Snake
S. s. blanchardi	Trans-Pecos Ground Snake
S. s. gloydi	Grand Canyon Ground Snake
S. s. isozona	Great Basin Ground Snake
S. s. linearis	Vermilion-lined Ground Snake
S. s. semiannulata	Santa Rita Ground Snake

STILOSOMA — SHORT-TAILED SNAKES

S. extenuatum	Short-tailed Snake

STORERIA — BROWN SNAKES AND REDBELLY SNAKES

S. dekayi	Brown Snake
S. d. dekayi	Northern Brown Snake
S. d. limnetes	Marsh Brown Snake
S. d. texana	Texas Brown Snake
S. d. victa	Florida Brown Snake
S. d. wrightorum	Midland Brown Snake
S. occipitomaculata	Redbelly Snake
S. o. obscura	Florida Redbelly Snake
S. o. occipitomaculata	Northern Redbelly Snake
S. o. pahasapae	Black Hills Redbelly Snake

TANTILLA — BLACKHEAD SNAKES AND CROWNED SNAKES

T. atriceps	Mexican Blackhead Snake
T. coronata	Southeastern Crowned Snake
T. eiseni	California Blackhead Snake
T. gracilis	Flathead Snake
T. nigriceps	Plains Blackhead Snake
T. n. fumiceps	Texas Blackhead Snake
T. n. nigriceps	Plains Blackhead Snake
T. oolitica	Rim Rock Crowned Snake
T. planiceps	Western Blackhead Snake
T. relicta	Florida Crowned Snake
T. r. neilli	Central Florida Crowned Snake
T. r. pamlica	Coastal Dunes Crowned Snake
T. r. relicta	Peninsula Crowned Snake
T. rubra	Big Bend Blackhead Snake
T. r. diabola	Devil's River Blackhead Snake
T. r. cucullata	Blackhood Snake
T. transmontana	Desert Blackhead Snake

T. utahensis	Utah Blackhead Snake
T. wilcoxi	Chihuahuan Blackhead Snake
T. w. wilcoxi	Huachuca Blackhead Snake
T. yaquia	Yaqui Blackhead Snake

THAMNOPHIS — GARTER SNAKES AND RIBBON SNAKES

T. brachystoma	Shorthead Garter Snake
T. butleri	Butler's Garter Snake
T. couchi	Western Aquatic Garter Snake
T. c. aquaticus	Aquatic Garter Snake
T. c. atratus	Santa Cruz Garter Snake
T. c. couchi	Sierra Garter Snake
T. c. gigas	Giant Garter Snake
T. c. hammondi	Two-striped Garter Snake
T. c. hydrophilus	Oregon Garter Snake
T. cyrtopsis	Blackneck Garter Snake
T. c. cyrtopsis	Western Blackneck Garter Snake
T. c. ocellatus	Eastern Blackneck Garter Snake
T. elegans	Western Terrestrial Garter Snake
T. e. biscutatus	Klamath Garter Snake
T. e. elegans	Mountain Garter Snake
T. e. terrestris	Coast Garter Snake
T. e. vagrans	Wandering Garter Snake
T. eques	Mexican Garter Snake
T. e. magalops	Mexican Garter Snake
T. marcianus	Checkered Garter Snake
T. m. marcianus	Checkered Garter Snake
T. ordinoides	Northwestern Garter Snake
T. proximus	Western Ribbon Snake
T. p. diabolicus	Arid Land Ribbon Snake
T. p. orarius	Gulf Coast Ribbon Snake
T. p. proximus	Western Ribbon Snake
T. p. rubrilineatus	Redstripe Ribbon Snake
T. radix	Plains Garter Snake
T. r. haydeni	Western Plains Garter Snake
T. r. radix	Eastern Plains Garter Snake
T. rufipunctata	Narrowhead Garter Snake
T. sauritus	Eastern Ribbon Snake
T. s. nitae	Bluestripe Ribbon Snake
T. s. sackeni	Peninsula Ribbon Snake
T. s. sauritus	Eastern Ribbon Snake
T. s. septentrionalis	Northern Ribbon Snake
T. sirtalis	Common Garter Snake

T. s. annectans	Texas Garter Snake
T. s. concinnus	Red-spotted Garter Snake
T. s. fitchi	Valley Garter Snake
T. s. infernalis	California Red-sided Garter Snake
T. s. pallidula	Maritime Garter Snake
T. s. parietalis	Red-sided Garter Snake
T. s. pickeringi	Puget Sound Garter Snake
T. s. semifasciatus	Chicago Garter Snake
T. s. similis	Bluestripe Garter Snake
T. s. sirtalis	Eastern Garter Snake
T. s. tetrataenia	San Francisco Garter Snake

TRIMORPHODON — LYRE SNAKES

T. biscutatus	Lyre Snake
T. b. lambda	Sonoran Lyre Snake
T. b. vandenburghi	California Lyre Snake
T. b. vilkinsoni	Texas Lyre Snake

TROPIDOCLONION — LINED SNAKES

T. lineatum	Lined Snake
T. l. annectans	Central Lined Snake
T. l. lineatum	Northern Lined Snake
T. l. mertensi	New Mexico Lined Snake
T. l. texanum	Texas Lined Snake

VIRGINIA — EARTH SNAKES

V. striatula	Rough Earth Snake
V. valeriae	Smooth Earth Snake
V. v. elegans	Western Earth Snake
V. v. pulchra	Mountain Earth Snake
V. v. valeriae	Eastern Earth Snake

The above checklist is excerpted from *Standard Common and Current Scientific Names for North American Amphibians and Reptiles,* published by the Society for the Study of Amphibians and Reptiles, Department of Zoology, Miami University, Oxford, Ohio 45056. © 1978 by the Society for the Study of Amphibians and Reptiles.

The publication is the work of an ad hoc committee composed of Joseph T. Collins, James E. Huheey, James L. Knight, and Hobart M. Smith. The purpose: to clarify and stabilize the use of names by the herpetological community and the general public.

LITERATURE CITED

BOBROWSKY, KENNETH. "Albinism in Reptiles." *Bulletin of the New York Herpetological Society*, Vol. 2, No. 3 (1965).

BURGHARDT, GORDON M. "Chemical Perception in Snakes." *Psychology Today*, August 1967.

CONANT, ROGER. *Field Guide to Reptiles and Amphibians of Eastern Central North America.* Houghton Mifflin, 1975.

DITMARS, R. L. *The Reptiles of North America.* Doubleday, Doran, 1907.

———. *Snakes of the World.* Macmillan, 1931.

———. *Reptiles of the World.* Macmillan, 1936.

DUNSON, W. A., ed. *Biology of Sea Snakes.* Baltimore University Park Press, 1975.

FRYE, FREDRIC L. "Role of Nutrition of Captive Reptiles." California Veterinary Medicine Association, Annual Seminar, 1974.

GOIN, COLEMAN J., and OLIVE B. *Introduction to Herpetology.* Freeman, 1971.

HEATWOLE, H. "Voluntary Submergence Times of Marine Snakes." *Marine Biology* 32 (Springer-Verlag), 1975.

IONIDES, C. J. P. *Mambas and Man Eaters.* Holt, Rinehart and Winston, 1965.

KAUFFELD, CARL. *Snakes and Snake Hunting.* Doubleday, 1957.

———. *Snakes? The Keeper and the Kept.* Doubleday, 1969.

KLAUBER, L. M. *Rattlesnakes.* 2 vols. University of California Press, 1956.

LEVITON, ALAN E. *Reptiles and Amphibians of North America.* Doubleday, 1972.

MARCUS, LEONARD C. "Diseases of Snakes." *Bulletin of the New York Herpetological Society*, Vol. 8, Nos. 1–2 (1971).

MINTON, SHERMAN A. and MADGE R. *Giant Reptiles.* Scribner's, 1973.

MORRIS, RAMONA and DESMOND. *Men and Snakes.* McGraw-Hill, 1965.

PARKER, H. W. *Snakes: A Natural History.* British Museum, 1977.

POPE, C. H. *Snakes Alive and How They Live.* Viking, 1937.

———. *The Reptile World.* Knopf, 1955.

———. *The Giant Snakes.* Knopf, 1961.

PUNAY, E. Y. "Commercial Sea Snake Fisheries in the Philippines." W. A. Dunson, ed., *Biology of Sea Snakes*, 1975.

SCHMIDT, K. P. and INGER, R. *Living Reptiles of the World.* Doubleday, 1957.

WYKES, A. *Snake Man: C. J. P. Ionides.* Hamish Hamilton, London, 1960.

Index